MARY TONETTI DORRA

beautiful american
vegetable
gardens

PHOTOGRAPHS BY STEVE ELTINGE

CLARKSON POTTER/PUBLISHERS   NEW YORK

*Preceding page: A central allée divides the vegetables from the roses in Linda Allard's walled garden.
Espaliered pear trees along the back wall are underplanted with hundreds of tulips, as is the main arbor.*

Copyright © 1997 by Mary Tonetti Dorra
Photographs copyright © 1997 by Steve Eltinge

Published by Clarkson N. Potter, Inc., 201 East 50th Street, New York, New York 10022. Member of the Crown Publishing Group.
Random House, Inc. New York, Toronto, London, Sydney, Auckland
http://www.randomhouse.com/
CLARKSON N. POTTER, POTTER, and colophon are trademarks of Clarkson N. Potter, Inc.

Printed in China
Design by Platinum Design, Inc. New York City

Library of Congress Cataloging-in-Publication Data is available upon request.

ISBN 0-517-70304-1
10   9   8   7   6   5   4   3   2   1
First Edition

To Henri, Amy, and Helen, who have each helped make this book come to light

ACKNOWLEDGMENTS

The writing of this book has been a real adventure! It has taken me into America's history and into towns, cities, countrysides, and villages all over the nation and into 10 of the 11 zones on the USDA Hardiness Zone Map. I invite the reader to share my adventure and visit some of America's most beautiful vegetable gardens. It is hoped that the profiles of the gardeners and their gardens will provoke a sense of shared experience and a fuller vision of America today in all its diversity.

I would like to express my heartfelt thanks to all the garden owners and their gardeners who gave so generously their time, their hospitality, their encouragement, and their enthusiasm, and who opened their gardens to me. And special thanks to Gordon and Anne Thorne and Susie Russell, whose wonderful gardens had to be deleted for lack of space.

To Jane Montant, former editor-in-chief of Gourmet magazine, who was the first to plant the seed for this book, and to Noel Young, publisher, who first recognized the subject would be worthy of a book.

To Helen Pratt, my agent, whose knowledge and patience were invaluable.

To Steve Eltinge, whose beautiful pictures added immeasurably to this book and whose intelligence, professionalism, and sense of humor made it a pleasure to work with him.

To Lauren Shakely, my editor, whose thoughtful, intelligent editing is equaled only by her sensitivity and understanding, and to Diane Frieden, assistant editor, whose painstaking editing is enormously appreciated.

To those who helped in finding or otherwise introducing me to the wonderful vegetable gardens of America: Ricky Allen, Valli Arader, Daphne Bertero, Barbara Bradley, Leslie Clapp, Robert Dash, Dorothy DiCecco, Kim Dougherty, Anita Engle, Susan Everitt, J. Barry Ferguson, Virginia Gardner of VLT Gardner Botanical Books, Paul and Alma Gray, Peter Hatch of Monticello, Mrs. Carl Hosmer, Margo Jacqua, Betty and Bob Johnson, Kristan Johnson of Abundant Landscape Design, Maxine Johnson, Ike Kirschner at Longwood Gardens, Ann Lester, Fran Levitt, Elise Lufkin, Laurie McDonald Meigs, Polly Moore, Sally Murphy, Sally Nordstrom, Dean Norton at Mount Vernon, Cynthia Nolen, Mary Novack, Steve and Maria Nygren, Mead Palmer, Kirsten Peckerman, Jane Pepper and Flossie Narducci of the the Pennsylvania Horticultural Society, Barbara Robinson, Jean Sherrill, Jack Staub, Mary Jo Strawbridge, Sarah and Virginia Weatherly, Jean Woodhull, and the Garden Club of America, Visiting Gardens Committees, in California, Connecticut, Georgia, Indiana, Iowa, New Mexico, New York, and Washington.

And special thanks to those who, in addition to the gardeners themselves and some of the above, extended gracious hospitality during the research and photographing of the book: Ann Aldrich, Madelaine and Dino Anagnostopoulos, Nina Kivelson Auerbach,

Mindy Black at Monticello, Phebe Bowditch, Hilda and Jack Doane, Wendy Foster, Jill Jakes, Elena Kingsland, Diana Neeley, Renny Reynolds, Marilyn and Charlie Schubert, Bill and Virginia Urschel, Chris and Alan Willemson, Bob and Mary Jane Woodward, The Hon. Robert F. Woodward, and Evans Woollen.

And for encouragement or other special help along the way:

To Julia Child, Joanna Barnes, Wendy Minot, and Senga Mortimer

And to Beth Benjamin, Kate Stadem and Renee Shepherd of Shepherd's Garden Seeds, Jan Blum of Seeds Blum, Richard Bowditch, Gary Coull of Johnny's Selected Seeds, the Dumbarton Oaks Library staff, Bob Boomsma of L.L. Olds Seed Company, Steve Blondo and Steve Rouhan of Gurney's Seed & Nursery Co., Laurie Hannah, librarian at the Santa Barbara Botanic Garden, Harlan Hamernick of Bluebird Nursery, Linda Harris of Ferry-Morse Seed Co., Tom Johns and Joel Reiten of Territorial Seed Company, Judith Jones, Tania Martin of the CED Library, University of California, Berkeley, Rose Marie Nichols McGee of Nichols Garden Nursery, Dick Meiners of Pinetree Garden Seeds, Sheperd Odgen of The Cook's Garden, Linda Sapp of Tomato Growers Supply Company, Carol Swift and Robin Worcester.

CONTENTS

3

THE MIDWEST:

LESSONS OF THE PRAIRIE 101

4

THE FAR WEST:

THE ULTIMATE MIX 135

A BEAUTIFUL VEGETABLE

GARDEN GUIDE 169

INTRODUCTION

"Americans will habitually prefer the useful to the beautiful, and they will require that the beautiful should be useful."

ALEXIS DE TOCQUEVILLE, *DEMOCRACY IN AMERICA,* BOOK III, CHAPTER 11

merica is currently reviving a tradition that goes back to the days when its early European settlers depended on the family's vegetable patch for survival and, at a later date, when the likes of George Washington and Thomas Jefferson took pride in aesthetically designed, well-tended, beautifully situated, and productive vegetable gardens. Gardeners are rediscovering the delights to be derived from creating and cultivating vegetable gardens that are at once beautiful and useful, and in so doing are giving new life to a long tradition of American design. And in the American melting-pot style, vegetables and flowers tailored to tastes and regional preferences succeed side by side with native sons.

The originality of American vegetable gardeners lies in part in their desire to harmonize the design with the topography of the land. The planting is generally best suited to the climatic zone of each garden. More often than not, the layout is related to the natural landscape, and reflects the vastness of the surrounding area.

In addition there is always a great emphasis on the practical and the useful: ease of access, ease of cultivation, the use of devices such as protective walls that will ensure the best growing conditions are always in evidence. The garden moreover must be a place where one enjoys rest and contemplation as well as the sheer joy of working in it. It must, of course, smell good too.

The vegetable garden above all is rarely isolated, or hidden away behind the house, as it was for centuries in Europe; in the United States it has often become the primary viewing spot of the site or rear of the property and has certainly been integrated into the total design. Finally, the exuberant combinations of colors; the informal mixing of flowers with vegetables, herbs, and shrubs; a certain boldness in the juxtaposition of shapes typical of many of the gardens in this book are all tributes to an independence of taste and a resistance to conformity in keeping with the American character. In 1914 Wilhelm Miller, when writing about Jens Jensen in *The Prairie Spirit in Landscape Gardening,* laid down the basic rules for the Prairie Style in landscape architecture. Little did he know that many of these same principles would be applied in the 1990s to a more general term: the "American Style" of gardening. Carole Ottesen in *The New American Garden,* published in 1987, further developed Miller's description of the emerging American style.

Perhaps the strongest early influences on American garden style are George Washington's Mount Vernon, and especially Thomas Jefferson's Monticello in Charlottesville, Virginia. Indeed, many of the gardeners in this book have said they make frequent pilgrimages to Charlottesville, in the spring or summer, in order to take inspiration from the combinations of vegetables as Jefferson himself conceived of them, from the splendid setting of the garden, and from the well-placed pavilion that offers maximum viewing delight.

The present gardeners at Monticello, under landscape director Peter Hatch, have meticulously re-created the vegetable garden according to Jefferson's careful notes and records in his *Garden Book,* a bible for some vegetable gardeners today. But even more important, it is Jefferson's humble philosophy ("But though an old man, I am but a young gardener") that gives solace to the new gardener in learning through continual trial and error. Jefferson's *ferme ornée,* or "decorated farm," as he referred to his property, overlooking his beautiful "sea view" of the misty Blue Ridge Mountains, gave American garden style its combination of beauty and practicality.

The vegetable garden at Mount Vernon in Alexandria, Virginia, has also been a source of inspiration. "The Lower Garden," as it was called when it was planned and planted by Washington in the 1790s, does not follow so religiously the historical model as does Monticello. While respecting as much of the original design as possible, Morley Jeffers Williams's design of the 1930s is typical of the Colonial Revival taste: a particular emphasis on making the garden perhaps even more orderly, even more beautiful than it was in Washington's time. According to Dean Norton, horticulturist at Mount Vernon, the neat parterres and grassy paths between them, the cordoned pear and apple trees along the walks, and the espaliered peach trees against the lovely brick walls, coupled with the subtle contrasts of textures in the plantings, make this garden one of the most inspiring examples of the Colonial Revival design, as well as one of the most beautiful in America. American vegetable garden enthusiasts intrigued by these space-saving techniques at Mount Vernon can appreciate the art of espaliered fruit trees at its best.

Another public vegetable garden that has proved to be both a source of inspiration and a font of technical information to creative gardeners is the demonstration vegetable garden at Longwood in Kennett Square, Pennsylvania. Thanks to the superb skills of Ike Kirschner, who is in charge of the vegetable garden, both new and experienced gardeners alike can learn new ways to grow vegetables organically and, in particular, intriguing methods for growing tomatoes, of which there are 70 varieties.

Finally, the gardens of Colonial Williamsburg, Virginia, in the context of the re-created village, contribute in their own special way to the historical perspective. After World War II, the exodus to the suburbs, as well as the marked jump in the population's longevity, resulted in a substantial rise in home gardening, making gardening the number one hobby in America. And the new enthusiasm was not limited to suburbia: many a townhouse garden now boasts its own vegetables, and numerous apartment dwellers with terraces and balconies have created sophisticated gardens, many of which include vegetables in planter boxes or pots. Simultaneously, growing concerns about the possibly excessive use of pesticides and fertilizers in commercial produce, and a revived insistence on freshness, have fostered new incentives for home vegetable gardening.

The rebirth of the vegetable garden coincided with the renaissance in American cooking of the past few decades. Once Americans began to have fun in the kitchen with Julia Child and other television cooks, they also learned to appreciate fresh produce and exotic vegetables that did not appear in local markets. In the 1960s, great chefs all over the country introduced a revolutionary change in the makeup of their menus, moving vegetables from their subordinate role as "side dishes" to starring roles complementing the main course. The plate became a perfect composition of subtle flavors, each enhancing the other, and vegetables claimed their rightful place in American cuisine.

As health-consciousness continues to grow, vegetables dominate the dietary pyramid.

The revolution in vegetable gardening owes a great deal to the scientific, industrial, and commercial communities. Botanists who have been investigating new species and old, in university, government, and industrial laboratories, have done much to improve the stock and available varieties. Chemists and manufacturers have introduced numerous products that make gardening more rewarding. A number of seed companies (see Source List), furthermore, are now providing seeds from around the world, as well as American heirloom seeds for the ever-curious, ever-experimental, enterprising gardener.

Above all, a tribute must be paid to the ingenious and hard-working gardeners who have learned to grow the vegetables most appropriate to their own region and best suited to their taste, and who have paid as much attention to the visual delight occasioned by a beautifully planned and carefully tended vegetable garden, as to the culinary appeal of its harvest. While most of the vegetable gardeners whose creations are presented in this book are not vegetarians, they would probably concur with Thomas Jefferson, about whom his niece Ellen Randolph wrote: "The little meat he took seemed mostly as a seasoning for his vegetables."

Those who tend the gardens featured in this book share with many other gardeners today, as well as with their American forefathers, in the belief that vegetables can and should enhance the beauty of a garden, much as they do the beauty and taste of a dinner plate. It is in implementing this belief, with dedication and humility, a lot of hard work, great sensitivity to local conditions, and the imperatives of their own tastes, that they have contributed to the evolution of an American garden style as well as to the delights of the American table.

1

NEW ENGLAND

"The essence of the enjoyment of a garden is that things should look as though they like to grow in it."

BEATRIX FARRAND, "A TALK TO A GARDEN CLUB," SEWICKLEY (PA.), JUNE 16, 1916

Hardy Garden Traditions

espite the fact that Celia Thaxter of New Hampshire has long been recognized as New England's most celebrated gardener (*An Island Garden,* her classic book illustrated by Childe Hassam, was published in 1894), perhaps no one typifies the garden traditions of New England more than Beatrix Farrand. Although she also gardened in California at the beginning and end of her life, Farrand made one of her most important gardens on Mount Desert Island off the coast of Maine, and she gardened there until she died in her eighties in 1959.

Farrand's contribution to the vegetable gardens of the region was that she believed their design to be just as important as that of the flower garden. When she laid out the plans for the garden of her aunt, Edith Wharton, at The Mount in Lenox, Massachusetts, she immediately dealt with Wharton's first priority—the kitchen garden.

Today's Northeast gardeners face the same climate and terrain that both encouraged and threatened their ancestors—zones that fluctuate from 5 in the hills to 7 in the valleys, often rocky but also often rich soil, and wind and sand along the coast.

An Impressionist Garden

A PRETTIER VEGETABLE GARDEN CANNOT be found than Beth Straus's "Somes Meadow" on Mount Desert Island overlooking Somes Harbor in Maine. The garden is a well-painted picture of beautifully grown vegetables, including peas, both bush and pole varieties; Swiss chard, beets, carrots, and cucumbers; tepees of melons and beans; at least five varieties of lettuces planted every two weeks; and especially a collection of alliums that happily cohabit: scallions, leeks, shallots, and of course several varieties of onions, including the huge and highly successful 'Lancastrian' variety, and 'Ebenezer', known for its long-storing capabilities—all basic necessities for the Straus kitchen.

According to Celia Thaxter's garden records, the painterly bouquet in the Straus garden would have been found in Thaxter's New Hampshire coastal garden over a century ago: love-in-a-mist, lilies, sweet peas, larkspur, hollyhocks, coneflowers, foxgloves, marigolds, phlox (both *Phlox paniculata* and *P. suffruticosa* varieties), verbena (*Verbena bonariensis*, *V. speciosa*, and *V. venosa*), and most important for the poetry of both the Thaxter and the Straus gardens: poppies, poppies, poppies!

(*Papaver orientale*, *P. somniferum*, and *P. nudicaule*). In addition Beth Straus has a few not found in the Thaxter garden: blue and white delphiniums, nasturtiums, scabious, snapdragons, nicotiana (*Nicotiana sylvestris* and *N. havana* 'Appleblossom' varieties), and colewort (*Crambe cordifolia*) that hovers for a good part of the summer season as a mist of blossoms over white and pink cosmos. The vegetables and flowers all share the background of the beautiful Somes Harbor that reaches through the pine-studded Acadia National Park on the only fjord of the North American coastline.

Beth Straus has much in common, both in her gardening philosophy and in her life, with Beatrix Farrand, also of Mount Desert and one of America's foremost landscape architects. Beth Straus believes, as Beatrix Farrand did, that the remarkable Maine landscape must be respected and preserved—indeed it was a source of inspiration for many of the latter's garden designs. Beth and Don Straus put an easement on the land between their house and the harbor to Acadia National Park to keep it forever wild. In so doing they continued a strong Maine tradition of land preservation established by the gifts of

Above: *Steve Hansen, who helps gardener Joy Lyons in the Straus garden, checks the large 'Lancastrian', or "football," onion that does so well in northern zones. Joy starts long-day bulbing onions from seed, then transplants them into 4-inch pots in the greenhouse to get an early start for Maine's short season.*

Pansy borders, daisies, and a row of lilies along the back fence brighten this section of the spring garden before summer vegetables mature. 'Lancastrians' usually need cool nights and 95 long days to reach their average 5-pound size. Right: Hummingbird faucet handles add an elegant touch to this orderly, unassuming garden.

Preceding pages: Beth and Don Straus look over their vegetable garden onto Somes Harbor and Acadia National Park. The vegetable garden, formerly a tennis court, is filled with well-cared-for vegetables and many old-fashioned flowers: foxglove, love-in-a-mist, sweet peas, daisies, phlox, and verbena. The central path is lined with marigolds. Some of the slats in the wooden fence have been removed to increase the air circulation and add to its rustic charm. Above: Nasturtiums, larkspurs, lilies, and delphinium make up the Impressionist palette in a corner of this island garden.

Charles W. Eliot, George B. Dorr, and John D. Rockefeller, Jr., founders of the park, whose goal was "to make the Park what it should be—a demonstration school for the American to show how much he can add to the beauty of Nature. . . ." As for her own garden, Beth Straus feels strongly that to bring in European accessories and artifacts, statuary, fountains, and anachronistic formal garden schemes would be "simply silly."

Planting is delayed until after Memorial Day in this short-season, long-day summer garden, where everyone agrees the plants "look as though they like to grow in it." Most of the annuals and the vegetables are started in a local greenhouse where the Strauses rent space in early spring to ensure that their plants will be ready for transplanting in June. Don Straus remarks, "You can practically hear the young plants panting to catch up once they've been put in the garden." It doesn't take long to catch up because the soil has been so enriched with composted manure that the young plants are happily on their way.

Like her Mount Desert predecessor Beatrix Farrand, Beth Straus acknowledges the importance of a vegetable garden. For Beth Straus the vegetable garden was also the first priority and the first garden planted in the landscaping of their house in 1978. The original part of the Strauses' historic house dates back to the 1780s and was later used as an inn for the early "rusticators," who began coming to Mount Desert Island chiefly from Boston and Philadelphia in the 1860s and 1870s. Mostly members of the clergy and educators, the early summer visitors were, in Dorr's words, "the brainworkers of the country, people who would be responsive to the beauty and inspiration of its scenery. . . ." Twenty years ago the Strauses responded much the same when they first arrived in Somesville and began the renovation of their house and garden.

"I didn't want to change the character of the place by interrupting the view with the vegetable garden. But the only flat area out of sight and in full sun was where the inn's clay tennis court had been," Beth explains. The problems were enormous. The clay of the court had to be scraped up as much as possible, and later raised beds had to be made with quantities of new soil brought in to create a depth of only 3 feet. The first garden was like most of those belonging to the Maine farmers, with a few flowers and basic vegetables for the family table. "I liked the way they just dig up an oblong and put it right out there in the middle next to the house and grow vegetables and flowers in the same patch. It is so simple and straightforward. So Mainey! I thought it looked wonderful," Beth admits.

ONIONS

Onion, Shallot (*Allium cepa*), and Scallion
(*A. fistulosum*)

Onions are either bulbing or "bunching" (the latter grow in bunches from the base of the edible stems). They can take 130 days to mature, making for usually only one crop in the northern zones.

WHEN
Start bulb onions from sets or seeds in the greenhouse in Pro Mix around Valentine's Day (as do Joy Lyons and Beth Straus in Maine).

WHERE
Light, sandy, well-drained, and already well composted soil is ideal. Rotate plantings from year to year.

HOW
Plant from seed (for greatest varietal choice), from prestarted plants (easiest), or from onion sets (small seedling bulbs already started whose growth has been interrupted). Use bonemeal when planting to stimulate bulb production.

CARE
Keep soil well cultivated and weed free; give plants a good watering at planting time and 1 inch per week throughout the growing season. After plants have grown a few inches, trim the tops to encourage root growth. When plants mature in late August, let them cure.

The Straus garden not only continues the unpretentious Maine tradition but does so in the context of a spectacular view. It is also unique because it is such a personal garden, with the special color and textural combinations that Beth Straus's artistic eye brought to the site. She and her gardener, Joy Lyons, have improved the original garden through annual experimentation and have dealt with the problems that only trial and error can solve. The powerful winds, for example, proved to be the worst enemy, necessitating a change from the simple chicken wire fence to a cedar one. In the eight years since the installation of the fence, some of the slats have been removed, providing more air circulation and a more informal look than a solid wooden fence provides. Beds of dahlias and other perennials were added at the time of the new fence along the eastern and western sides. As the Strauses, like many of their rusticating predecessors, increased their annual stay on the island from a few weeks, her bountiful bouquets in the house required more late-summer varieties and more flower beds were added. Another bed was dug near the original section of the garden specifically for herbs, many of which winter over. But the vegetable garden itself remained a little smaller than the former tennis court: 80 feet by 64 feet. Although the garden is neat and orderly, its asymmetrical layout is anything but formal—in keeping with the Maine tradition that inspired the first Straus vegetable garden. The marigold-lined path does not divide the garden equally: for practical purposes the large central section for the vegetables and annuals is on one side so they can be easily rototilled twice a year. The perennials, which include delphiniums and phlox, are on the other side. Anchoring the corners are perennial stands of lovage (from which Beth makes a marvelous soup with the onions from the garden), dill, and perennial crambe.

Because of the harsh Maine winters, only the hardiest perennials are cut back to about 2 inches, covered with a layer of hay to prevent the heaving caused by alternate thawing and refreezing of the soil, and topped with evergreen boughs to keep the hay from being blown away by the wind. Otherwise almost the entire garden must be started afresh annually. Nasturtiums growing upward on a tepee mark the end of a colorful row of ruby chard. Tomatoes run along the length of the back fence, and the well-behaved cucumber vines are kept neatly tucked into one of the corners, out of the way of the space allotted to the eggplant nearby.

Beth Straus grew up with her mother's beautiful garden in Belvedere, California, and brings her love of art, extensive travel experiences, and a familiarity with European gardens to the design of her own gardens on Mount Desert Island. "Having a garden was just a way of life in California. We more or less lived in the garden. For me it is very difficult to think of living without flowers. For thirty years Don and I didn't have a garden. I was frustrated, so that is why I went to work as a hands-on volunteer at the New York Botanical Garden and took gardening classes from T. H. Everett, who wrote the *Gardening Encyclopedia*." She credits the former director of horticulture of the New York Botanical Garden with having started her 50 years ago on the way to becoming a passionate practicing gardener. ⚞

Right: A "bean harp": vertical strings tied to a wooden stake across the top offer support for the string beans and form a lace-curtain effect on the northern side of the garden. If amply watered and if harvested regularly, the pole beans provide for the entire season.

Exotic Greens off the Coast of Maine

"I DON'T HAVE TOO MANY THEORIES about vegetable gardening. It's just something I have to do. Gardening is in my genes," Jan Moss declares. Although she lives in New York City during the winter months, where she has no garden, her garden in Maine is always with her, and wherever she has lived, gardening has been an important part of her life. "But it wasn't until twenty-five years ago," she admits, "when I came to Cranberry Island, that I could garden to my heart's content, and that's what I've done ever since I've been here."

Like clockwork, in mid-September anything that has not been eaten is turned under and the garden is put to bed. "If I have straw I put that on top of the freshly turned soil, and sometimes a cover of seaweed, rinsed of salt, is laid on top for the winter." Unlike many gardeners in zone 5, where for eight months the winters don't permit gardening of any kind, Jan Moss continues to garden even after she returns to her Manhattan apartment— both in her mind and more recently on her computer.

When the Mosses first acquired their property in 1971, Jan started digging in the garden even before she was completely unpacked. That first garden was only 3 feet wide and 8 feet long. Today there are several carefully planned flower and foliage gardens on their 2-acre island property, but the favorite is still the vegetable-dominated first one near the kitchen door, the one that is most visited for its culinary treasures and most admired from the terrace. The vegetable garden has grown during the past decades from "a few petunias and lettuces" in a 3-by-8-foot plot to a 30-by-60-foot garden of tremendous edible variety and ornamental richness—despite its still manageable size.

Not only does the list of vegetables change every year, but the planting scheme is also varied according to new discoveries and challenges. In keeping with Jan's appreciation of the natural beauty of the plants themselves, there are very few garden accessories. Nothing could be more appropriate than the pergola-like structure at the bottom of the garden made by Jan's husband, Fred Moss. Posts from their native cypress trees and decorative pieces of driftwood collected on the beach support an extremely floriferous clematis and provide a stunning focal point for most of the summer. A lavish border of Japanese irises flanks the archway and wraps around the eastern

Above: Jan Moss grows many old-fashioned flowers that appropriately complement her Victorian summer home. Poppies of all kinds including Papaver somniferum make a colorful show year after year. When Jan found the deer didn't like them, they became an even more important addition to her garden. Using computer programs such as Fractual Design "Dabbler" and Microsoft "Paintbrush" enables Jan to redo her garden each year. While keeping favorite flowers and vegetables such as poppies and Asian greens on the computer screen, she can "paint" new design ideas, incorporating new plants into the scheme during the planning stage in January.
Right: Fifteen minutes before supper Jan gathers Mizuna and other greens for stir frying and for salads.

ASIAN GREENS

Nonheading Asian Cabbage (*Brassica rapa*, Pekinensis group) and Asian Greens

Most Asian greens are early, fast-growing (45 days), cool-season vegetables that are one of the first greens to appear, and as a fall crop, one of the last to leave.

WHEN
Direct-seed or start in the greenhouse (as is done for Jan Moss's garden in Maine), allowing plants to grow strong for a few weeks before putting them in the garden in early June.

WHERE
Most plants will grow in hot weather and are fairly drought and shade tolerant; they enjoy well-drained, fertile, sandy soil.

HOW
Sow seeds in the ground as early as it can be worked. If transplanted from the greenhouse or flats, plants should be set about 8 inches apart.

CARE
Keep Mizuna and other *B. rapa* varieties moist during the growing season. When direct-seeded, all nonheading cabbages can be harvested as needed. Pull the small, flat rosettes at thinning time, leaving larger rosettes (6–8 inches apart) to be harvested when they reach their full 12 inches across. Plant Chinese spinach every 2 weeks for a continuous supply to mix with salad greens all summer.

side of the garden, reminding one of Jan Moss's insistence that the vegetable garden is a thing of beauty as well as source of food for the table.

To less experienced gardeners, the short season may seem very limiting, but Jan's years of experience in this charming island garden off the coast of Maine have taught her that she has a tremendous freedom of choice: "I've tried almost every vegetable that will grow here, and though there are some vegetables we would never be without—such as a few of the Asian greens, lettuce, tomatoes (especially the heirloom striped German ones from Johnny's Selected Seeds), squash, kale, and arugula—every year there is something new to be tried or retried in a different way. Several years ago I edged an area in the back garden with carrots. I have also used red kale, regular kale, parsley, and lettuce in the same way." Recently the flat cabbage, Tat Soi (available from Johnny's Selected Seeds and Shepherd's Garden Seeds; see the Source List for addresses), provided a beautiful edging of low-growing, flowerlike rosettes. The emerald green Tat Soi leaves are spoon shaped and account for one of the translations, "gourd ladle vegetable," of this slightly bitter stir-fry green that is becoming more and more popular with American gardeners.

For Jan a flurry of activity begins no later than May 20. "When I arrive on the island I begin by removing the nontillable seaweed that was left to add nourishment to the soil during the winter. [It will later be used for mulch.] Then I rototill in some packaged manure, and finally I add a wonderful new discovery for me, an organic fertilizer from Gardens Alive [see Source List]. It makes everything in one week's time just burst forth." Once the soil is ready, the vegetables are planted directly into the ground: peas, carrots, beets, broccoli raab, beans, several varieties of lettuce, kale, chard, and most of the Asian greens. Flowers such as delphinium that are

Above: *Across the lawn at the far side of the Moss garden stands one of the sculptures made by Gary Allen, a local craftsman who uses wood from cypress and alder trees on the island. He and his wife, Colleen, start Jan Moss's seedlings in their greenhouse at Cabin Creek Farm.*

grown as annuals, the newly introduced annual holly-hock, and some of the other vegetables such as broccoli, Japanese eggplant, and tomatoes are grown from seeds that Jan sends in February from New York to local gardeners Elaine Fernald and her sister Joanne Fletcher ("There is nothing they can't grow better than anyone, and this is done in portable cold frames!"). Colleen and Gary Allen of Cabin Creek Farm, located on the island, also help get her seeds started early in the greenhouse. Jan allows an extra month in the flats, as this seems to make the plants even stronger when they are finally ready to be put into the ground in mid-June. She has learned from experience to plant only what she and her family can eat during the four months on the island and what they can't find in the supermarket.

Mizuna, also known as Kyoto greens (*Brassica rapa* group *Japonica*) is another favorite that is successively planted and continues to look beautiful all summer. It grows very fast to about 2 feet high. Jan prefers it when it is only about 8 inches tall, but she can continue to harvest throughout the summer even when it is fully grown, as she cuts from the center where it is still very tender.

Mizuna provides a constant, imaginative, and easy source of "something to eat" as a mild-flavored stuffing for chicken and fish or more simply in a mixed summer salad or a stir-fry.

Jan depends on other exotics in the brassica family such as Hon Tsai Tai (*Brassica rapa* var. *purpurea*), a beautiful purple nonheading cabbage that sends up pencil-thick shoots with tender purple leaves and will continue to do so if it is not allowed to produce its lovely golden flowers. Other strong accents of purple and red are found in the red orach 'Orach Crimson Plume' (*Atriplex hortensis*) and in red Russian kale (*Brassica oleracea*), both of which are planted in diamond-shaped sections that zigzag between clumps of rich dark green Swiss chard and the small, strikingly serrated leaves of Shungiku, or chrysanthemum greens.

A 3-foot-wide path separates the above bed from another rectangular patterned bed where rows of 'Lemon Gem' marigolds colorfully divide the broccoli raab from clumps of feathery Mizuna and Hon Tsai Tai, offering a pleasing textural contrast as well as their glorious color combinations. Over the years Jan has grown other members of the brassica family, including the rich green Bok Choi, or thick mustard cabbage that resembles Swiss chard; and the hybrid Pak Choi—both the green-stemmed Mei Qing Choi and the white-stemmed Joi Choi are hybrids offered by Johnny's and Shepherd's in their seed catalogs. They are always delicious in stir-fries, or, in a more westernized tradition, Shepherd's suggests sautéing them quickly in butter or braising them in broth as a side dish.

Two other greens add to the beauty of Jan Moss's garden: *Amaranthus tricolor* and the *Chrysanthemum* greens mentioned earlier. The latter, also known as chop suey greens or Shungiku (*Chrysanthemum coronarium*), are a little too pungent for eating once they have started to blossom into their daisylike flowers, but take center stage as a summer bouquet. But even more important than their decorative asset, it is the tangy taste of their leaves in a salad, soup, or one-dish sukiyaki or simply steamed that assures them a place every year in Jan's garden. Her other favorite for its visual and gustatory delights is the spectacularly colored *Amaranthus tricolor* (syn. *A. gangeticus*), also known as Chinese spinach. This leafy amaranth is not to be confused with the grain or decorative amaranth despite its name and family connections. The one in Jan Moss's garden is the leafy vegetable whose tender red leaves can be used in salads, soups, or stir-fries and is especially good in a risotto with porcini mushrooms. In some areas (not Maine!) it can easily become a weed if allowed to flower and drop its seeds, but if it is kept in check it is a fine addition to any ornamental vegetable garden. Jan placed it next to bright yellow calendulas in an exceptionally pleasing color combination.

The Asian greens that so uniquely characterize this garden were planted, Jan says, because they come up so fast and "you can always have something fresh to eat at a moment's notice." But equally important, the exotic greens symbolize, in a way, her extraordinary curiosity about and special passion for all growing things. "In Asia, and particularly in China, one eats a lot of very unusual things. I like to try them out of curiosity for the taste, but I am also curious to see if they will grow here." It is, in part, this curiosity that makes her a great gardener. The gardening tradition in America will always be alive and thriving as long as there are gardeners like Jan Moss whose curiosity, energy, and passion are focused on creating and experimenting in the garden.

Left: *A "must" for Jan's garden is the decorative Asian cabbage 'Joi Choi' from Johnny's Selected Seeds.*

Right: *The garden has grown "from a few petunias and lettuces" to a 30-by-60-foot rectangular plot producing a variety of vegetable and flowers. "Deer didn't bother 25 years ago, but all of a sudden they started coming and the fence didn't keep them out at all; it had to be heightened and laced with wire."*

The Uninterrupted Garden

AN 18TH-CENTURY FRENCH TRAVELER described a road north of Boston, not far from Essex, Massachusetts, as "an uninterrupted garden. . . . The road is in every part better than any I have ever seen in America. It would be considered a delightful road, even in the most beautiful districts of France and England." Today garden visitors from abroad are just as impressed by American gardens and particularly by the gardener who takes advantage of the site. Mrs. Evelyn Bartlett, who is 108 and has accumulated 60 years of gardening experience on her present 110-acre property, has indeed turned her farm into "an uninterrupted garden." At Bothways Farm, Mrs. Bartlett and her able gardener, Karl Kohring, can grow just about any vegetable they have a mind to. While celery, for those who grow it at all, is usually harvested in August, at Bothways Farm having celery for Thanksgiving dinner is an annual challenge they know how to meet. (See Growing Tips from the Gardeners for Karl's secret.)

By the first of August an abundance of fruits and vegetables are picked: tomatoes, eggplant, peppers, summer squash, a continuous crop of string beans that had been planted at regular intervals, corn, and even a second crop of kohlrabi that is up and coming along. Mrs. Bartlett happens to like kohlrabi—a misunderstood but mineral-rich vegetable. Kohlrabi is planted to be harvested both in early June and then again in early September to take advantage of the cooler seasons because the kohlrabi bulbs will split in the hot summer months.

When Karl first came to Bothways Farm he spent eight hours a day weeding. "There's got to be a better way," he thought at the time. No mulch had ever been used. The soil was so porous that the water disappeared faster than it was coming out of the sky and the weeds kept coming up continuously. When he became head gardener, one of the first things he did was enhance the poor, sandy soil with compost and wood chips from a tree service looking for a place to dump their shavings after a pruning job. "It was amazing what this did for the soil. The wood shavings made the nicest topsoil you can imagine and added the organic material needed to build it up. At the same time, the soil became immediately more

Above: *Karl Kohring uses the large greenhouse built in the 1920s for starting celery plants and other vegetables as well as during the winter months for protecting the citrus trees shown here in whiskey barrels. Wide* *flagstones line the 100-foot walkway that stretches the length of the garden. Right: Everyone enjoys the fresh fruits and vegetables. Rams and exotic animals including ostriches share the pastures with the cattle.*

CELERY

Celery *(Apium graveolens* var. *secalinum)* and Celeriac or Celery Root *(A. g.* var. *rapaceum)*

Celery and celery root grow best when given lots of time to mature (120–130 days) at a mild temperature of around 70 degrees.

WHEN
Gardeners in warm-summer climates should start plants in August. For a late October harvest, sow celeriac seeds in early July (as Karl Korhing does at Bothways Farm).

WHERE
Plant in rich, balanced, and consistently moist soil in a location that receives 6–8 hours of sun each day.

HOW
Novices should set out seedlings from a local nursery. Seeds can take as long as 25 days to sprout; start those as early as February or March.

CARE
Protect roots from early frost by covering them with straw or other organic mulch. To encourage larger bulbs, enrich the soil with liquid fertilizer once a month during the growing season. Add extra phosphorus to the fertilizer at planting time for excellent results. Water regularly during the growing season.

moisture-retentive, so it wasn't necessary to water as often." Weeds were kept to a minimum by keeping the soil mulched. In fact, the labor-intensive activity of weeding and watering was reduced by half. There had been many bald spots in the garden, which meant another place to lose moisture (and to grow weeds!). Today these bald spots are practically nonexistent because Karl began staggering the rows of vegetables—depending on the amount of space they required—in a 2–1 or 3–2 pattern. He had devised an ingenious planting grid of 32 by 32 inches (made of a few boards and woven cattle fence wire nailed together). Laying out the 150-foot-long garden became a much easier job. The vegetables are still planted in rows, but these are much wider, and the whole effect is beautifully symmetrical as long as he keeps his lines straight (which he does with string). When the vegetables start to grow, a natural blanketing effect of the almost-touching foliage helps prevent the weeds from emerging.

Evelyn Bartlett's farm is a summer picture of American abundance at its best: eggplant, squash, towering poles of tomatoes hanging from the vine, and numerous other plants make up a straightforward combination of well-grown vegetables. On both sides of the central path of the garden, a brilliant display of hundreds of zinnias and other summer flowers—including a second burst of 6-foot-tall delphiniums, gladioli, dahlias, foxgloves, hollyhocks, and other perennials—add to the beauty of the whole garden.

Right: A sampling of the vegetables from the garden that Karl Kohring arranges three times a week for the kitchen at Bothways Farm.

Cape Cod Classic

THE GARDEN OF PAUL AND RACHEL LAMBERT Mellon on Cape Cod at Osterville, Massachusetts, is like many American gardens on the eastern seaboard today. It echoes the values and taste of their 18th-century American predecessors in its characteristic formal layout, simplicity, and restraint. Because she loved the surroundings of her house on Cape Cod, Rachel "Bunny" Mellon wanted to keep the naturalness of the place foremost in the garden design she laid out 30 years ago: the reconstruction of sand dunes that had been swept away, the planting of dune grasses to preserve them from erosion, the views of the water inlets from the terrace, and the native trees surrounding the property were all major elements in her original plan. A short distance from the main house a tall privet hedge encloses the vegetable garden, protecting it from the nearly hurricane-force winds that terrorize summer gardens on Cape Cod. The hedge also secludes from view the stunning array of flowers and vegetables that, however useful and beautiful they might be, if not set quietly and distinctly apart would otherwise intrude on the natural beauty of the surrounding landscape. This sensitivity to the beauty of nature around her

has earned Bunny Mellon the respect of such foremost professional landscape designers and architects as Daniel Urban Kiley, who proclaims: "She is brilliantly skillful as a designer and has exquisite taste."

Although never formally trained as a professional garden designer, Bunny Mellon has acquired her knowledge and skills over a lifetime, through prodigious reading and studying, through careful observation of other gardens when traveling, and most of all through working in the garden herself. "I gardened with my grandfather when I was a little girl and at fourteen I designed my first garden. All my life I have worked in gardens. It has become second nature to me and I never tire of doing it." The vegetable garden at Osterville demonstrates her horticultural and design skills, although she modestly insists the garden is "not an important garden, nor is it special," adding, "I love this garden because it is useful."

Six immaculate white gates, chest-high and simply yet elegantly decorated with narrow spools and hand-hewn finials, offer convenient access through the tall privet hedge that surrounds the approximately 115-by-84-foot garden. Cheerful, welcoming, and very informal clumps

Above: *One of the four flower beds in the central section of the Mellon garden provides ample cutting flowers for the house, including achillea, marigolds, and white and blue salvia.* Right: *Occasionally, holes in the garden need filling in, and plants are kept in the greenhouse for that purpose. After renewing the beds, Lisa Rockwell replenishes the tender seedlings in carefully laid out rows where needed. Planting goes on at intervals throughout the summer for a continuously beautiful and productive garden.* Overleaf: *Wide grassy paths separate the 12 beds that form a somewhat symmetrical arrangement. As the summer progresses, flowers spill onto paths, creating a more informal look. The white beamed structure at the right is a mesh cage protecting the tomatoes from the birds.*

Above: *There are enough lettuces to share with some of the wild creatures who find the large variety too tempting to resist.*

of Shasta daisies are clustered near the entrance. Nearby, in two of the eight beds devoted exclusively to flowers— as important to the Mellon household as the vegetables—are the tall towers lifting to higher levels soft pastel sweet peas, coveted for their gentle fragrance. The sweet peas are but one of the many plants chosen for their scent. At twilight especially, the air is perfumed by tuberoses and sweet peas, the faint scent of herbs intermingling.

The planting scheme makes this one of the most beautiful vegetable gardens in America. Here vegetables, flowers, and herbs are artfully intermixed in a series of 12 beds geometrically ordered and punctuated only by a

sundial and a much-frequented birdbath. Vegetables planted in straightforward rows and a continuous profusion of flowers give the impression of a deceptively simple garden. Yet the garden is well thought out in every detail, carefully timed and exquisitely executed by Lisa Rockwell, the head gardener at the Mellon estate.

The garden is also distinguished by its restraint and understatement. In 1993 it was reduced by half, in keeping with the Mellons' desire to grow only what they could comfortably use. Bunny Mellon's original garden plan, with its central axis and intersecting wide grassy paths, has remained the same. Only the beds at the back have been reduced or eliminated and replaced by a small orchard of cherry, nectarine, plum, and peach trees and different varieties of apple. A new large grassy area provides a peaceful oasis from summer heat.

At the other end of the garden are two hexagonal gazebos, one used for the drying of flowers for winter arrangements and the other for storing garden tools. In between them a shingled Cape Cod–style utility building serves as an office for Lisa and her gardening team of seven. The office is flanked by two greenhouses kept at different temperatures, where most of the seeds are started and other plants are wintered over. (They also house the herb topiaries that have become one of Bunny Mellon's signatures in her interior designs.) The beautiful bell-shaped roofs of the gazebos were inspired by the traditional 18th-century colonial design that one occasionally sees on garden structures in the South, particularly in Virginia (the schoolhouse at Mount Vernon and the Tayloe office at Colonial Williamsburg).

Lisa Rockwell, a graduate in floriculture from North Carolina State University, is the gardening magician who arranges to fill the garden with glorious produce-to-come once the Mellons and their family are in residence for the summer. Most of the vegetable seeds are selected from the Burpee's or Shepherd's seed catalogs (see Source List), but some are brought back from the Mellons' travels in Europe. Through meticulous record keeping and good gardening intuition, Lisa schedules the sowing of seeds and the transplanting of vegetables from the cold frame into the garden so that the family can count on a continuous production of vegetables at the peak of perfection from the end of June until the end of September.

Though "a simple country garden," the Mellon vegetable patch yields a spectacular variety of well-grown vegetables. Planted in orderly rows in the four main

CAULIFLOWER

(Brassica oleracea)

Like cabbage and broccoli, cauliflower is a cool-season crop. In most parts of the country it is best grown as a fall crop.

WHEN
For a spring crop, start seeds April 1 in clay pots in the greenhouse instead of flats (as Lisa Rockwell does in the Mellon garden in zone 5). The daytime, outdoor temperature for seedlings should be a minimum of 50 degrees. In mild winter zones, plant in late autumn for an early-spring harvest.

WHERE
Plant in soil with a high pH, afforded by a good dose of lime at planting time.

HOW
When seedlings have 2 sets of leaves, transplant them to peat pots and harden them off in the cold frame for a week. In mid-May, or when daytime temperature has warmed to at least 50 degrees, take the plants (still in the peat pots, which will disintegrate in soil) and place 15–18 inches apart.

CARE
Blanch to keep the heads white only if necessary (that is, if the variety is not self-blanching, such as Burpee's 'Early White Hybrid') by wrapping leaves around the heads while they are still small. Tie securely with string.

vegetable beds, they are arranged so that the textures as well as the colors of the foliage make an appealing arrangement even before the vegetables are ready to be harvested. Alabaster 'Early White' cauliflower (one of the family's favorite vegetables) does amazingly well in zone 7 ("the last place to warm up in the spring and the last place to cool down in the fall," says Lisa) when she gets it off to an early start before the heat of summer takes its toll. Another crop is planted at the end of June along with broccoli, Brussels sprouts, kale, and cabbages so that there will be one more harvest before the Mellons leave in September.

One of the most attractive and prolific vegetable beds is bisected by a tall wire trellis that gives the garden another dimension and provides support for 'Streamliner', 'Sweet Success', 'Early Pride', and 'Burpee Hybrid II' cucumbers, all from the Burpee catalog. On either side of the cucumber trellis, planted 2 to 3 feet on center according to the space needed, are rows of sorrel, cauliflower, celery, broccoli, onions, beets, fennel, squash, lima beans, and green and yellow beans—all running perpendicular to a wide, colorful border of pink zinnias, pink-and-white cleome, dark blue salvia, and a kaleidoscope of colorful "candy lilies" (*Pardancanda* × *norrisii*). These unusual lilylike flowers are actually in the iris family and come in warm orange, yellow, and coral tones from Park Seed (see Source List); here, they attractively embellish the golden 'Butterstick' squash on the vines creeping next to them. Different floral arrangements of annuals and perennials in the other vegetable beds, too various to mention, have been selected for their visual compatibility in brightening the rows of vegetables as they are making their way to full summer or fall fruition. Feathery dill and lady's mantle often relieve

the sturdier textures of the chard, celery, broccoli, and kale. When a harvested vegetable leaves a blank space, a plethora of fillers is waiting in the cold frame: among them cosmos, nigella, or a new variety of marigolds. 'Aurora' and 'Gypsy Sunshine' marigold did well their first year in the garden.

Finally, looking across the garden one sees a rectilinear mesh cage on sturdy slim wooden posts protecting from birds and other wildlife a collection of absolutely perfect tomatoes: 'Burpee's Early Pick VF Hybrid', 'Big Girl', 'Lady Luck', and 'Better Boy'. They, and the two 'Sweet 100' tomato towers nearby, are never rotated like the other vegetables and have now become permanent fixtures.

Although it is a feature of a summer residence, the Mellon garden is a working one. "The more I garden, the more I learn. It never stops," Bunny Mellon says. Nor does Bunny herself when it comes to designing gardens for her own pleasure and delight or that of her friends.

Right: *The 20-foot-long tomato cage where four varieties of tomatoes grow year after year.*

Color by Design

IT WAS ROSEMARY VEREY'S BARNSLEY House in England that was the inspiration for the large (90-by-120-foot) walled garden of the fashion designer Linda Allard in Washington, Connecticut. Here, vegetables, herbs, flowers, shrubs, and trees grow together harmoniously. Linda explains, "I saw Barnsley House about three years before I started my own house. Just thinking about having a garden like that pushed me into buying the property where I could have a beautiful vegetable garden."

Taking her cue from the formal design of Verey's kitchen garden, Linda laid out her own vegetable garden so that it could be best appreciated from her second-floor bedroom window, as formal French gardens were meant to be viewed from the public rooms on the first (American second) floor. Facing east so that the sun falls on them all day long, the formal squares, circles, and other path-defined formal patterns are laid out along a central axis. While the overall layout shows the hand of a skilled designer, an even more remarkable aspect of Linda Allard's garden is her carefully orchestrated planting scheme, which ensures an almost miraculous state of constant renewal.

Because of the garden's continuous beauty, Linda's two seasonal goals are a surprise: "I try to get the garden finished by the middle of June so that I can relax for a while, and then get the winter crops in by mid-July." Nonetheless, from May through November an abundance of ripening fruits and vegetables has been carefully planned to replace those that have been harvested, and the promising beginnings of more to come are always reassuringly visible. "The garden is planted so fully that it is a surprise later in the season to find it so changed from the 'limitations' of the earlier hard-edge design." The first spring lettuces, carrots, and beets emerge in *L*-shaped blocks or trapezoidal beds that flank the carefully laid out circles and squares. Magnificent rows of early tulips, cherry blossoms, and tripods of English peas go by almost unnoticed after they have reached their early-spring peak, as they are eclipsed by the orderly curves of lavender, chives, strawberries, and oncoming cabbages interplanted with bouquets of feathery dill and bright

Above: *A most formal allée of climbing roses separates the vegetables from the roses in this large Connecticut walled garden. Bold triangular patterns are formed in the herb sections by the steppingstones left over from the house construction. Cosmos grow in the fernlike foliage of the long asparagus bed next to the arbor.*

Right: *Eggplant blossoms in summer provide an additional accent that fits in appropriately with Linda Allard's color scheme of lavenders, purples, mauves, and reds in her choice of vegetables, herbs, and flowers.*

Left: 'Racambole', or 'Stiffneck', garlic (Alium sativum var. ophioscorodon) creates varied patterns and strong green and white contrasts among the more traditional foliage of the herb garden. It is available through Johnny's Selected Seeds.

Right: Italian putti are very much at home in the garden of this Tuscan-style villa designed by Linda Allard's brother David Allard. Opposite: Gertrude Jekyll could have been describing Linda's garden when she said: "The pictorial art of Botticelli is everything that the architects claim for the formal garden; it is full of sweetness and beauty, full of limitations, frankly artificial, frankly artistic."

Above: *The stone wall surrounding Linda Allard's garden offers protection against the wildlife and is a buffer against strong winds that so often plague gardeners high on the hillside. Tools and garden equipment are stored in the sheds in the northern wall.*

blue bachelor's buttons or the dramatic display of climbing roses and clematis that cover the 14 central arches in mid-June. Through successive plantings of several varieties of onions and leeks, Linda's kitchen is constantly supplied with this important staple. Her cookbook *Absolutely Delicious* is filled with recipes inspired by the vegetables from her garden.

In 1991, when the house was finished, Linda established the structural design of the garden. Each year since then she has approached the planting schemes in much

the same way she begins to design her newest fashion collection: freethinking sketches evolve into final colored drawings of the whole garden. She laughingly admits that often the colors in her garden are influenced by those she used in that season's collection.

One of Linda's favorite vegetables is the parsnip, which can be very tricky to grow. "The difficulty is in the germination, so I try to follow the recommendation of my uncle Stanley. He told me to put a piece of wood or moist burlap on top of the parsnip seeds to keep them damp until they begin to sprout. I plant them in clumps of four or five seeds about four inches apart. Rarely do they all germinate, but I thin them to only one strong plant anyway. The 'All-American Parsnip' from Nichols Garden Nursery and 'Lancer' from Johnny's Selected Seeds [see the Source List for addresses] are my favorites. I direct-seed enough of them in early May so that some plants are left in the ground until after a frost or two, when they get a special sweetness just as do the turnips and Brussels sprouts." Requiring close to 100 days from planting to harvest, parsnips are almost always in the garden and often next to clumps of bachelor's buttons. The gray-white bachelor's button foliage offers protective shade while the parsnips are getting started, and later the combination with the beautiful dark green parsnip foliage creates a particularly compatible textural background for the eye-catching blue flowers.

The color combinations throughout the garden reflect the artistic flair of the talented designer. Each year there are new experiments with color, forced to a certain extent by the necessity of rotating the vegetables. In one year a strong purple and red emphasis meant various kinds of eggplant, including the pinky purple 'Neon' variety from Johnny's, the deep purple 'Violetta Lunga' from The Cook's Garden, and both the elongated Japanese variety 'Asian Bride' and the darker-toned 'Rosa Bianca' from Shepherd's Garden Seeds. These shades are echoed in the neighboring purple basil and peppers, and in the red, violet, and purple pole beans ('Scarlet Emperor' from Nichols, 'Trionfo' from Johnny's, and 'Purple Pod' from Henry Field's Seed & Nursery in Shenandoah, Iowa) growing up the handsome green 8-foot metal *tuteurs*. Also growing up these trellises are purple, magenta, and red clematis ('Royal Velvet', 'Niobe', 'Ville de Lyon', 'Mme. Julia Correvon', 'Mrs. N.

PARSNIPS

(Pastinaca sativa)

The parsnip can be very tricky to grow, as seeds are slow and difficult to germinate and it takes 100–110 days from planting to harvest. Parsnips do not do well in excessively hot weather but do need warmth to fully develop.

WHEN
For a continuous crop, begin direct-seeding as early in May as the ground can be worked (as Linda Allard does), and sow seeds again around Memorial Day, and finally in late June for a late-fall harvest—a frost or two will bring a special sweetness to those plants left in the ground. In mild-winter zones, parsnips planted in late summer are left in the ground for a continuous winter and early-spring harvest.

WHERE
Soil should be deeply cultivated and composted and kept evenly moist and weed free.

HOW
Plant in clumps of 4–5 seeds about 4 inches apart. Thin to only one strong plant. Alternatively, plant seeds liberally, ¼–½ inch deep, then thin when 1 inch tall to about 4–5 inches apart. Germination can take as long as 3 weeks.

CARE
Once established, fertilize once a month in addition to a 5-10-5 fertilizer worked in at planting time.

Thompson' and 'Dr. Ruppel'). Strong horizontal dashes of lavender mark the ends of the rectangular beds. Elsewhere in the garden, deep violet pansies edge the onion squares, a clump of bright red dianthus skirts the gray-green leeks, scarlet-tinged beet leaves accompany purple-topped turnips, red radicchio stands next to a curving row of purple cabbages, and garnet stalks of ruby chard and rhubarb continue the theme. Sweeps of chives with a few lavender heads left on for color wrap around the main circular bed, and elsewhere dots of tiny red alpine strawberries edge a carefully planned bed of tarragon and basil.

But color combinations are not all that dictates the garden's companion plantings. A particularly successful grouping of vegetables is that of the cucumbers planted between two rows of beans to share the same tepees. The beans do not overly shade the cucumbers, and, in fact, the cucumbers rather like to be shaded as they begin their vertical climb. Their vines will keep the tepees covered and replace some of the pole varieties once they have been harvested. The cucumbers will continue to share the tepees with the later varieties of shell beans until frost.

Sunflowers coming through the tomatoes provide a delightful combination of summer color once the tomatoes are in fruit. Deep red 'Empress of India' nasturtiums run alongside the tomatoes, making a felicitous contribution long after the tomatoes have gone by and well after the first frost.

Most of Connecticut is in zone 6. Linda Allard's garden, however, beautifully situated high on a hill overlooking her apple orchard and the valley below, has the disadvantage of dipping into zone 5, with lowered temperatures and the additional hardship of strong winds

that can be devastating to a garden. "I knew I wanted a walled garden for aesthetic reasons," Linda explains. She realized a wall would contribute significantly to the formality of the design by delineating the outer limits of the garden and would support the espaliered apple trees as well. But even more important, the wall provides much-needed protection from the wind and from the deer and other wild animals that would otherwise ravage the garden.

Linda's passion for gardening and cooking obviously means a lot of hard work. She is used to that, having been taught since childhood that hard work pays off. In addition to teaching their children good gardening principles and a love of cooking and gardening with friends and family, Linda Allard's parents were responsible for a few other important lessons. She strongly affirms one of the main principles of the idealistic American work ethic that built our country: "I think you can do anything you want to do if you just stick to it and work hard."

Opposite: For some, tulips are a sign of spring. They also signal it is time to plant parsnips, peas, spinach, and lettuce, which need a cooler season to get a good start. Linda Allard's collection of tulips and cool-season vegetables are given the best beginning in well-composted, well-prepared soil.

A Garden Within a Park

IT IS DIFFICULT TO SAY WHICH IS MORE important to Juanita Flagg: her enormous trees that contribute so generously to the sylvan parklike setting of her 11-acre property in Middletown, Connecticut, and which were planted largely by Juanie herself over the past 30 years—or her beautiful vegetable garden that for years fed her family of four children. Only once did these two horticultural loves—the trees and the beautiful vegetable garden—come into conflict. Twenty-five years ago Juanie realized that the peonies and some of the vegetables were getting too much shade from the huge sugar maples on one side of the 80-foot by 40-foot vegetable garden. The remedy was fairly simple: she simply moved the vegetable garden farther into the sun, where the once-shaded peonies began to thrive. They now form an enchanting peony walk along the vegetable garden's western side, starting at the entrance.

Maples, beech, and oaks make a spectacular annual autumn show in the woodland, and green shade in full summer. The summer harvest includes tomatoes, chard, onions, eggplant, peppers, and beans. But Juanie particularly loves her garden in the springtime, when dogwood and cherry trees, along with peonies, lilacs, and tulips, burst into bloom, and asparagus, early lettuce, some herbs, and, of course, one of the earliest of all—spinach—make an appearance.

Juanie claims she learned to love spinach only after she tasted it just harvested from her own garden. She plants fresh seed as soon as the soil is workable in the raised beds, which she tries to get ready in the fall. Over the years she has grown many varieties, but she finds 'Melody' one of the most satisfactory. Both 'Melody' and 'Wolter' (whose smooth, dark green leaves contrast beautifully with the various spring lettuces) are planted right in the middle of the garden in a decorative pattern around a hexagonal-shaped center that is outlined in *fraises des bois,* the woodland strawberries.

She plants the seed thickly and uses the thinnings raw in salads, then regularly picks the spinach while it is still young and at its best. Juanie loves it cooked in every conceivable way—steamed, sautéed, creamed, or puréed in soups. Her favorite recipe calls for the freshest, tenderest leaves, which are washed and quickly sautéed in olive oil (or half olive oil and half butter) with a bit of garlic.

Above: *Behind the restored 1745 Connecticut farm-house, a formal vegetable garden and swimming pool are landscape focal points in Juanita Flagg's parklike setting.* Right: *The lavender blossoms of chives* *contribute a valuable ornamental touch and can be snipped for use in the kitchen to enliven many dishes both for taste and for decoration.*

Above: *Pale blues and grays, such as in this combination of crested iris* (Iris cristata) *and lamb's ears* (Stachys lantana), *are but one of the plant associations found in Juanita Flagg's garden. Opposite: Hostas, bluebells, and other bulbs and trees come to life in May.*

Juanie says the secret for growing vegetables that taste so good is in the soil. "Most of the soil in Connecticut is on the acid side, giving an additional advantage to vegetable gardeners in our state. No mineral additives are necessary, as the soil is naturally rich. I do increase the natural acidity of the soil around the blueberries each year, and we sweeten the soil with lime for all the herbs and even around the tomatoes." In March or as soon as the ground is no longer wet, she begins to add what she calls "solid gold manure," which allows her to have a bumper crop of vegetables without rotating crops each year. The manure is sparingly mixed in with thin third stage compost and is spread over the entire garden only once a year.

Deer have become a problem in many gardens all over the country and particularly in Connecticut, and Juanie's garden is no exception. Until recently, she always had Labrador retrievers around, and the dogs seemed to keep the deer away. Without them, even the steep ravine that separates the neighboring state park from her property is no deterrent to the increasingly brazen deer.

SPINACH

(Spinacia oleracea)

A cool-season vegetable, spinach is one of the joys of spring and fall before the garden is closed up for the winter. Growing time is usually 37–45 days.

WHEN

Plant as soon as the ground is workable in early spring (as Juanie Flagg does). Seeds can be sown in most zones at weekly intervals several times during the spring and again in late summer for a cool-season fall crop.

WHERE

Soil should be well composted and rich in humus. Spinach grows well in full sun that does not scorch; it will tolerate some shade.

HOW

Direct-seed 1–2 inches apart in rows 1 foot apart. When seedlings are 3 inches tall, thin plants to 5 inches apart. Thinnings are tender to eat; toss with salads.

CARE

Until seedlings are 3 inches tall, boost the soil regularly with liquid fish emulsion or kelp meal. Keep plants well watered and weed free. If the temperature is too hot (over 75 degrees), shade either with other plants or with shade cloths draped over hoops.

New Garden—
Colonial Roots

"MOST VEGETABLE GARDENS ARE RATHER dull, and that is why we set out to create something beautiful with the herbs, flowers, and vegetables we wanted to grow," says Jon Wood, who is part owner of Stone's Throw Gardens and Nursery in East Craftsbury, Vermont. His partner, Frank Oatman, explains that the basic concept for their garden was a Colonial American one, "inspired by those who wanted their vegetable gardens to be practical and productive as well as delightful to view and to stroll in. And those have always been our aims as well, ever since we first saw George Washington's Mount Vernon." They admired the many neat and well-tended home vegetable gardens so common in their northern Vermont area, but they felt that focusing too narrowly on vegetable production alone meant lost opportunities for making the vegetable garden a place of beauty. Frank adds, "[These home gardens] all seemed to cry out for a frame and a form within it."

The frame in this case is a fence with entrances on each of the four sides that cut through the old split-cedar rails. Weathered and covered with lichens and moss, the fence is very much in keeping with the Stone's Throw farmhouse

that dates back to 1795 and is typical of those used in rural Vermont at that time. The fence surrounds a 35-by-70-foot rectangle that Frank and Jon carefully planned for shape and size. It has remained basically the same since first planted in 1974, although the vegetables are rotated and the flowers are apt to change from year to year.

Inside the fence, vegetables are laid out in formal, raised plots along four main paths, with the main quadrants divided into beds of very exact short rows. "We have found that simply raking up the soil into these raised beds keeps the soil light and uncompacted," Jon says. "Once the soil has been well improved, no annual deep rototilling is needed. The slightly raised beds, formed only of raked-up soil (no edging), help to produce ideal drainage, too."

After seven years of experimenting with squares, triangles, and circles of various sizes, they settled on a circle with a 10-foot diameter as the most pleasing focus for the center of the garden. Four triangular beds flank the circle and are filled with a variety of vegetables and herbs planted in patterns to show off different textures and shades of green. These include Swiss chard, broccoli,

Above: *Stone's Throw Gardens in East Craftsbury, Vermont, shows just how pretty a vegetable garden can be. In late June, visitors are welcomed to the garden by two very large 'Festiva Maxima' white peonies and the first roses of the season. The tepee structures at the far end of the garden support English peas. Started indoors with many other vegetables, they* are transplanted on May 31, which is the traditional planting date for most Vermont gardeners. Right: *A detail of the Scotch thistle* (Onopordum acanthium), *which offers a strong architectural statement in any garden. Its cut flowers make stunning floral arrangements.*

BROCCOLI

Broccoli, Broccoli Raab, or Rapini *(Brassica oleracea)*, and Chinese Broccoli or Gai Lon *(B. o.* var. *alboglabra)*

Most members of the cole family are cool-season vegetables. Chinese broccoli, or Gai Lon, is early and fast growing. Italian or broccoli raab never forms a head, so the tender leaves and stems can be harvested longer. The growing season for first pickings is about 60 days.

WHEN
Set out in early spring after danger of heavy frost is past (Jon Wood and Frank Oatman start seeds under growlights in late March or April, then transplant to the garden by May 31), and again in midsummer, 2–4 months before the first frost.

WHERE
Plant in a sunny area in well-composted, rich soil.

HOW
Plant seeds ¼ inch deep in flats of prepared planting mix and cover lightly. Transplant seedlings to deeper pots when they have 2–4 sets of leaves; then harden off, and plant in the garden.

CARE
Keep young plants moist and weed free. Provide shade during the hot months, and shield fall seedlings from frost with a floating row cover or a glass cloche. Some side-dressing or a second fertilizing is often necessary for broccoli after plants are well established.

broccoli raab, Chinese or Gai Lon broccoli, leeks, chives, oregano, chervil, dill, basil, and parsley. Successive plantings of short rows of lettuce tucked in here and there provide just enough salad greens to feed them and their many guests and, at the same time, prolong an attractive design for the whole summer. From the end of May until early September the garden is productive and "delightful to stroll in." Radishes replace the early spinach; peas (both the old-fashioned shelling variety and snow peas), lima and 'Great Northern' bush beans, 'Early Boy' tomatoes, 'Green Comet' broccoli, peppers, eggplant, and cabbage are constantly maturing, being harvested, and replaced with new plants, continuing a pleasing tapestry effect from spring to early fall.

The central bed is encircled by a bark-covered path setting off a variety of seasonal flowers planted in concentric circles. Bunched together with early tulips, alliums, and nicotiana are lilies—both Asiatic and Oriental hybrid varieties—some of which stretch the season into late summer and perfume the garden with their delightful scent. Cutting through the central bed are gray-white spokes of dusty miller *(Artemisia stellerana)* that divide the circular bed into eight radial sections. These represent the eight right-fold paths of Buddhism, a philosophy espoused by the garden owners. The spokes all point to the center, which is punctuated by a tall flagpole waving a large colorful flag with an orange dragon on a yellow and orange field, in tribute to the Republic of Bhutan, the owners' favorite winter destination spot.

The colors of the Bhutan flag declare the palette of the garden—warm tones of yellow, orange, and red that are accentuated by an occasional spike of blue delphinium or bushes of *Baptisia* (false indigo) covered with vibrant purple flowers at the back (southern) entrance. All of the paths are lined with complementary low-growing annu-

Left: *Since colonial times, cabbages have been a mainstay of the Vermont vegetable garden. The purple variety 'Cardinal' from Harris Seeds is a zone 3 favorite.*

Right: *Blueberries grow outside the main vegetable garden along with gooseberries and the more rambling squashes. At Stone's Throw the highbush blueberry hybrids 'Bluecrop' and 'Blue Ray' are two varieties that grow well in zone 3 in a soil that has a low pH (4.5–5.5).*

Above: A pile of Vermont fieldstones separates the large 'Celsiana' Damask rose on the right from 'Jens Munk', a Hybrid Rugosa rose. In the background is a resting place from which to admire the peonies Jon and Frank offer for sale at their nursery. Right: F. Jon Wood II and G. Frank Oatman, Jr., are shown here with their own hybrid, 'La Duchessa de Alba'.

als, such as ageratum, alyssum, and small marigolds. In addition, the vegetable triangles and concentric circles of flowers in the center have for many years been outlined by the small English daisy (*Bellis perennis*), which together with the well-tended bark paths creates a strong geometric pattern for the entire garden—the "form" within the frame.

In about 1980, along the outside of the fence on the western side, Jon and Frank began what is today a spectacular collection of shrub roses, a particularly appropriate background for a delightful country vegetable garden. Among their favorites are 'Alika', a hardy Russian Gallica Grandiflora that covers itself with brilliant red blossoms once a year; and the striped Gallica 'Rosa Mundi'. The scented 'Blanc Double de Coubert', a Hybrid Rugosa, and the old rose Harrison's Yellow are both hardy shrub roses that withstand zone 3 well.

But perhaps the most striking floral decoration of the garden—and the owners' favorite flowers—are the peonies. In spring the visitor is formally welcomed at the main (northern) entrance to the vegetable garden by two very large 'Festiva Maxima' white peonies. Next to them on either side is a gloriously long row of peonies ranging from deep mauve to pale pink ('Longfellow', 'Richard Carvel', and 'Sarah Bernhardt').

All the space-consuming squash, including 'Delicata', buttercup, zucchini, cocozelle, and the yellow crookneck, are grown beyond the fence, where their vines have ample room to wander and sprawl near the highbush blueberries, gooseberries, raspberries, and apple trees—the latter known since the 18th century as one of Vermont's prides.

Sunflowers interplanted randomly with the rows of beans offer a touch of color and whimsicality in the otherwise formal layout. When they mature they reinforce the importance of height, and balance at the other end of the garden the 9-foot towering Scotch thistle (*Onopordum acanthium*), whose strong architectural statement adds a note of drama for the entire summer.

Another vegetable block is on the western side in front of the 7-foot-wide perennial border that dramatically asserts the bright colors of summer and magically follows the paler shades of spring without missing a beat. It consists entirely of potatoes: 'German Fingerling', 'Peruvian Blue', 'Yellow Finn', and other choice varieties. In spring this block is massed with bright purple blossoms and fairly shouts to its neighbor, the red 'Alika' rose.

In the 18th century, Vermont barns were typically two stories high and built on a hill reached by a ramp or "high drive" to bring the hay up to the second story so that it could be pitched down to the cows below. Although the original barn burned down decades before the present owners bought the property, Jon and Frank have cleverly turned the plateau at the top of the high drive into a viewing platform for their beautiful vegetable garden. The garden's exact site was determined by the spectacular view of the Vermont hills in the distance and of the soft meadows that have been seeded with native wildflowers close by the vegetable garden.

While Jon Wood and Frank Oatman have looked back to the horticultural ideas and designs of Thomas Jefferson and George Washington for inspiration, they have also looked closer to home—at their picturesque Vermont hills, their 18th-century farmhouse, and their native plants. They sum it up well: "You've got to feel what each place is and what is special about it and bring new solutions to the place."

the MID-ATLANTIC and SOUTH

"Every house has its garden."

PETER KALM, 1791

Challenges and Solutions

throughout the colonies, and later in the early United States, a garden was so essential to survival that it was planted almost before adequate shelter was established on the property. Certainly the site of the garden frequently determined the location of the house. European visitors admired gardens of America for their productivity and practical designs, but they were also impressed with the beauty of the plants. From the beginning, America was a gardener's paradise.

In 1748 Peter Kalm (1715–79) was dispatched to North America by the Swedish government to explore the plants of the continent and to report his botanical findings to his teacher, the great Carl Linnaeus, whose system for the naming of plants is used to this day. Kalm was very much impressed with the gardens and farms he visited in New Jersey, and he reported his findings with great enthusiasm in *Travels in North America* (1770).

In the Mid-Atlantic and southern regions today, some gardeners battle with the heat and humidity of the summer months, but they also celebrate a wealth of cultural resources, from the black-eyed peas native to Africa to the red currants from Scandinavia.

Jungle
in the
Sky

THIS RUSTIC, PRODUCTIVE COTTAGE GARDEN resembles many others in its cheerful intimacy of flowers, vegetables, and herbs, but the one big difference— and this garden's glorious distinction—is that it flourishes high in the sky. In the Eichengreen/Bailey penthouse garden on the Upper West Side of Manhattan, the containers have been custom-made to fit into an irregular space, measuring a mere 325 square feet. At some points on the brick-walled terrace the width is less than 3 feet. Every square inch is ingeniously utilized to take advantage of the magnificent views of the New York City skyline or, on the western side, of the George Washington Bridge and the spectacular sunsets over the Hudson River. Even the sophisticated silver tomato spirals, supporting indeterminate fat red 'Supersonic' and 'Dona' varieties, are elegant echoes of the tallest vertical symbols of Manhattan in the distance: the Chrysler and Empire State buildings. Nearby are long clusters of 'Super Sweet 100' cherry tomatoes and their delicious little 'Yellow Pear' cousins making their own decorative and culinary contributions throughout the summer.

Laurie B. Eichengreen, a Manhattan-based landscape designer, specializes in penthouse gardens. Her own is an ongoing field of experimentation where, since 1979, she has tested new design ideas and has come to know the pitfalls of gardening in the sky. She has found, through years of experience, solutions for dealing with summer temperatures soaring into the 100s, the frequent high winds, and the sheer physical difficulties in transporting into the city and up to the 20th floor not only plants and their containers but bags of fertilizers, soil amendments, and the very soil itself.

Yet, even in winter, Laurie and her partner, W. H. Bailey, wouldn't have it otherwise. They see the city framed by evergreens and branches of 20-year-old clump birch, flowering cherry, and Japanese maple. The shades of periwinkle, lavender, and mauve in the chaise, bench, and dining table give this city garden a lift on overcast days. Many of the annual flowers and vegetables were chosen to echo the colors of the painted furniture: phygelius, 'Purple Splendour' brachycome (Swan River daisy), sweet potato vine, Chinese spinach, purple opal

Above: *Laurie Eichengreen chose blue-violet balloon flowers* (Platycodon grandiflorus) *to echo the lavender dining table. Various mustards and mescluns that have a purplish cast and purple-leafed opal basil are nestled into planter boxes.*

Right: *"Scumbling," a painterly term that dates back to the 17th century, begins with a thick impasto. Laurie's partner, W. H. Bailey, has created an antique effect on the wall beneath a rambling hydrangea vine.*

Left: *Laurie Eichengreen and W. H. Bailey look out their penthouse window over the tomatoes that climb stainless-steel spirals.* Above: *Bumblebees and ladybugs find solace in this garden in the sky.* Right: *Sunflowers crown a corner of the "yellow garden," which also includes dill, Jerusalem artichokes, coryopsis, and nicotiana.*

basil, and eggplant, to name a few, chosen for their specific shade of purple or lavender.

Espaliered and cordoned apple trees with numerous vines—climbing hydrangea, Boston ivy, trumpet, honeysuckle, and clematis—decorate the white and gray paint-scumbled brick walls. A collection of midsize shrubs, including a 'Bailey' blackberry bush, photinia, pyracantha, burning bush, and rhododendron, have been carefully chosen for their winter hardiness and appropriateness to scale. And finally, the most important foundation elements of this terrace garden in the sky are the permanent customized containers and the deep planter boxes. In winter a few of the terra-cotta pots, filled with dormant perennials, are buried in the soil of one of the planter boxes for protection against cracking during winter's freezing months. A winter crop of mesclun grows in the new portable cold frame that fits on top of another planter box. To these shrubs, vines, and trees that form the structure of the penthouse garden will be added young vegetable seedlings, a new supply of the necessary herbs Laurie can't do without in the kitchen, and new flowering annuals that she carefully selects and brings in to the city from favorite suburban nurseries.

Rectangular boxes enjoy the southern exposure and are filled with heat-loving tomatoes, space-saving pole beans (purple 'Dolichos' hyacinth and 'Blue Lake'), fennel, and an underplanting of *Laurentia axillaris*, the recently introduced blue starlike flower with feathery foliage that gives off a lovely gentle perfume after a spring shower. An old favorite climbing rose, 'Constance Spry', which dependably appears each Memorial Day weekend, is paired with a 17-year-old *Clematis × jackmanii*, whose purple blossoms intertwine with pink morning glories and bracket the kitchen window box of herbs and flowers.

Laurie admits, "I would have liked to have made the five-foot rectangular boxes a little wider, but the narrow walkway on the southern side determined their width." All of her containers must have good drainage

Above: *Hosta and dill are planted at the base of the not-quite-ripe 'Bailey' blackberries that climb up the penthouse's scumbled wall.*

holes on the bottom, and bricks or cleats are placed underneath the containers so that they have good aeration at the root level. Certain boxes are especially treasured because of the patina they have acquired through 17 years of use. The larger the container, the greater the soil volume, which means a better chance for plant survival in a severe winter.

No space is wasted. Even in their large boxes at the base of the trees underplantings of herbs and unusual new annuals are initially tested for Laurie's clients in her own penthouse garden, where they are commingled in a happy profusion of flowers, herbs, and vegetables. Yet scale is very important. She always has a variety of well-placed plants: low-growing, middle range, and tall ones to keep the garden from being single-leveled. In many cases smaller varieties of plants such as miniature roses, alpine strawberries, and dwarf snapdragons complete the picture more harmoniously than standards.

Since container gardening requires special care in watering, Bailey, who is responsible for this chore, prefers to irrigate with a can instead of a hose so he can tune into each plant's individual needs and at the same time take some quiet meditative time for himself. Generally, once-a-day watering during the height of summer is not too much, even though all the plants are mulched. And Laurie gives a good liquid fertilizing every two weeks to the tomatoes and once a month to the rest of the garden during the growing season.

But, just as necessary, the initial pot preparation that Laurie has devised over the years gets her vegetables and flowers off to a healthy start. She places a layer of ³⁄₄-inch gravel in the bottom of all containers—large and small— then a sheet of landscape fabric or even a simple fiberglass air-conditioning filter from the hardware store. This layer, one of the most important factors in lengthening the life of a wooden planter or window box, also keeps the roots from growing though the drainage holes (which would make the root ball harder to remove when the plants need potting up). Since the landscape fabric helps in lifting out the entire contents of a window box or shallow container, fall cleanup can be efficiently and neatly taken care of. "The soil must be changed or amended every year with humus, cow manure, at least a handful of vermiculite to retain water, and perlite for good drainage. I like a denser and heavier soil to keep the pots from tipping over in heavy winds," Laurie says.

While the terrace garden at first appears to be merely lush and full, a closer look reveals individual still-life compositions. One, in purple, lavender, and pink, is highlighted by new spring lettuces or the exotic purple-leafed *Perilla frutescens*, viewed in the window box outside a lace-curtained bedroom window—yet another example of Laurie's constant experimentation with the new and unusual. Perilla is known as *shiso* in Japan and is becoming more widely used in this country in cooking and as a decorative herb. It is available through Nichols Garden Seeds and Seeds Blum catalogs (see Source List for mail-order addresses).

Each of the colorful horticultural canvases in this rooftop garden is designed to be viewed not only from within but also as a backdrop for the superb urban views beyond. On the western side of the terrace the "yellow garden" is a breathtaking display at sunset. Shades of yellow, orange, and gold are represented by different varieties of coreopsis ('Moonbeam', 'Sunray', and 'Zagreb'), marigolds, and 'Stella d'Oro' daylilies mixed with the softening foliage and lacy yellow flowers of fern-leaf dill, which is always allowed to flower and go to seed for next year's still-life arrangements.

TOMATOES

(Lycopersicon lycopersicum)

Tomatoes come in early-, mid-, and late-season cultivars. The bush types are determinate, and they stop growing at a certain height and produce many tomatoes all at once. Vine-type tomatoes, indeterminates, are the best choice if space is limited because they grow vertically and produce fruit successively over a longer period of time. Plants take 68–78 days from transplant to maturity.

WHEN

Sow seeds indoors in flats or peat pots in a moist soil mix about 6 weeks before the last frost date.

WHERE

All tomatoes need the maximum amount of sunlight (6–10 hours a day) and loose, rich, slightly acid soil (pH 6.0–6.8).

HOW

Sprinkle seeds about ½ inch apart and cover with a ¼-inch layer of soil. Transfer to larger pots or thin to one strong plant when seedlings are 3–4 inches tall and have 2 sets of leaves.

CARE

Apply a weekly dose of liquid fertilizer (half to full strength) until seedlings are transplanted. Reduce watering and stop fertilizing after a hardening-off period to acclimate seedlings to outside temperatures. Once plants are in the garden, add mulch to keep the soil damp and weed free and to protect roots from burning during very hot summer months.

A Passion
for Peppers

ANN AND JOHN SWAN'S REPUTATIONS AS TWO of Pennsylvania's best gardeners are well deserved. They are particularly known for their unusual vegetable garden, which is dominated by an extensive collection of well-grown peppers. The vegetable garden is only a part of their 3-acre garden in West Chester, Pennsylvania, and was begun roughly 30 years ago when the Swans bought their untamed property and began to garden in a way that would years later bring them both blue ribbons at the Pennsylvania Horticultural Society's Harvest Show.

The vegetable garden covers about 1,900 square feet and was laid out on three 12-foot-deep, neatly cut terraces that represent a happy solution to one of the Swans' first gardening problems. "The site had since the American Revolution been a dumping ground for rubble from a nearby rock quarry. In the meadow garden area of our property, the rocks were thirty feet deep! We cleared away hundreds of rocks all by hand, just the two of us," John remembers. "And I still recall the back pains after all these years!" Despite the labor-intensive job of removing the rocks, filling in the remaining holes, and coping with the rather steep rise left by the excavation,

the site was nevertheless the best place on the property for a vegetable garden. It faced south, was in full sunshine all day, and was in full view from the patio deck for frequent admiration. The three terraces fit so gracefully into the overall garden that one is inclined to think they were created for aesthetic reasons alone and not merely to solve a grading problem.

The Swan garden is designed so that one area flows into another throughout the seasons. The vegetable garden, even though it is fenced to keep out four-footed pests, does not stand in isolated splendor, but is a part of the overall flower, shrub, and vegetable garden design and is a focal point to be admired from the patio. The entrance to the vegetable garden is boldly announced by two sentinels on either side of the gate: upright plumes of golden feather reed grass (*Calamagrostis* × *acutiflora*). In the spring, colorful bulbs, shrubs, and perennials are generously spotted in the beds just outside the fence that frames the vegetable garden, including the tiny-leafed lilac 'Miss Kim' and lilies—both the tiger (*Lilium lancifolium*) and the daylilies (*Hemerocallis*). In the late summer when the vegetables (and particularly the peppers)

Above: From the Ann and John Swan pepper collection are three of their favorites on top of the basket: 'Canary' (yellow and sweet), 'Ancho' (red and hot), and the tiny red Bird peppers (hot). Clustered below is an assortment of hot and sweet varieties, including the long yellow 'Super Sweet Banana', a pale green 'Cubanelle' (sweet), purple and green sweet bells, and elongated red 'Anaheims' (hot). Right: Ann and John harvest their West Chester, Pennsylvania, pepper patch in early September.

Above: *Tiny hot Bird peppers the Swans named for their friend Ethel Jane are similar to those commercially grown by Tomato Growers Supply Company, which are originally from Thailand and called 'Thai Hot'. Given the right conditions, even these hot varieties can be grown in colder zones.*

are taking center stage, most of the perennials have bloomed and faded, with the exception of an occasional radiance of an orange-yellow hybrid *Helianthus × multiflorus* 'Loddon's Gold' and clumps of phlox—both white and pale pink ones, which add gentle touches of color.

But the beauty of this vegetable garden is not dependent on its flowers—perennial or annual. Instead, the garden succeeds through the arrangement of the terraces and the varied composition of textures and shades of grays

and greens. Every element is carefully considered: the giant tasseled reeds in the background (*Arundo donax*) play off the feathery grasses (some striped and some bronzy red and some simply golden in the sunshine), and in the central part of the garden the Swans have created a broad tapestry of various textures in the lettuces, beans, squash, okra (both the burgundy variety and the ordinary green one), the startlingly green and white Bok Choi, bright red rhubarb chard, rosettes of Tat Soi, borders of golden thyme, and 2-foot-high emerald green basil plants. Enhancing the whole picture are the garden's stars—60 pepper plants with sparks of red, green, yellow, and orange flashing beneath rich green leaves.

The three terraces are bisected by a sloping grassy path leading up to an archway over the back garden gate. During the summer months the arch is covered with a mantle of lush green foliage, but in fall it becomes an even more important focal point of the garden when covered with small white blossoms of the fall-blooming sweet autumn clematis (*Clematis maximowicziana*). The grassy path bisecting the terraces is lined on both sides with railroad ties that offer a convenient seat for resting, smelling the herbs, and admiring the garden. Or, in full season, they serve as a ledge for the baskets used to gather the vegetables. Other railroad ties stretching the width of the terraces are used as paths so that foot traffic does not compact the soil. Since space is important in this small garden, the railroad ties afford an ideally narrow yet efficient access to the vegetables. The smooth weathered-gray surface presents an attractive visual contrast to the dark compost-laced earth and the various textures of the vegetable foliage. Today the central axis path adds to the beauty of the garden and offers a pretty separation of the hot peppers from the sweet ones so they "don't marry in the night," as Ann Swan says jokingly, "since they are apt to cross-pollinate if planted near each other. The hotter the peppers, the more apt they are to take over.

"Chili peppers that one is more apt to find in supermarkets today such as Anaheims and Anchos were practically unheard of in our area when we first began our garden," says Ann. "And it was because of our love for them in jellies, pepper sauce, and spicy ethnic food—particularly those like the Bird peppers I had grown up

PEPPERS

(Capsicum annuum, C. frutescens, C. chinense)

Sweet bell or fiery chili, peppers are a warm-season vegetable that grows anywhere that corn does. They require a long growing season (60–90 days) and are heavy feeders.

WHEN
Plant seedlings (started in the greenhouse or flats indoors in short-season areas) once the soil is well warmed up and nights are consistently in the 50s (usually mid-May).

WHERE
Soil should be slightly acidic to slightly alkaline (pH 6.0–8.0), well composted, and well drained.

HOW
Start seeds indoors 8–10 weeks before transplanting. Snip off all but the hardiest seedlings to leave one per pot. After hardening off, set peppers out 18 inches apart.

CARE
Protect peppers from wind and provide regular moisture during the growing season. Ann and John Swan's peppers benefit from heavy mulching with salt hay. (See "Protecting Young Plants" in Growing Tips from the Gardeners for John's method of using bottomless black plastic nursery pots to improve water retention and as cages for wind protection.)

Left: *From the top of the vegetable garden one looks through a bower covered with the fall-blooming 'Sweet Autumn' clematis (Clematis maximowicziana) down to the terrace below, where more perennials, shrubs, and grasses continue the integrated garden design.*

Right: *Red chili peppers such as the 'Ancho' can be as eye-catching in the garden as brilliant red flowers.*

with in Bermuda—that we were forced to find the seeds and grow our own." Today their pepper collection includes favorites such as the mild 'Cubanelle', 'Sweet Havana', 'Fushimi', and 'Pepperoncini' and the hotter types 'Copacabana', 'Jalapeño M', 'Serrano', 'Thai Hot', and the tiny hot Bird pepper 'Ethel Jane', named after the friend in whose garden the unnamed variety was found. Each year since 1980 they have continued to plant a few new test varieties as well as those they wouldn't be without. For lack of space the others that don't do well or that they don't particularly like have been dropped. Yet there are still more than 21 varieties in the garden today.

The Swans' gardening schedule begins in the fall. In late September, once they have harvested the last peppers and tomatoes, John and Ann begin their annual cleanup, removing all signs of the past year's vegetable garden. After all the salt-hay mulch is removed, the remains of the garden go to the compost pile, and John tills the earth, adding mushroom "soil" compost purchased from a nearby mushroom grower. If needed, he adds calcium.

By February, having pored over seed catalogs and gardening books during the winter months, the Swans have carefully selected and ordered their seeds (see Source List) to add to those that are commercially unavailable, such as 'Ethel Jane' and 'Australia', names they coined for unnamed varieties that they saved from the previous year's favorites. In early March they begin their indoor planting of peppers and tomatoes. During the first two weeks of May, they move the flats of seedlings outdoors to a wind-protected area in order to take advantage of the natural sunlight and to begin the new plants' "hardening off," or adjustment to the outdoor environment.

Each night the flats are returned to the warmth of the house, and by mid-May the young plants are put in the ground in plastic nursery pots along with the onion sets and seeds of carrots and basil—a necessary herb for Ann Swan's kitchen. The lettuces, peas, spinach, and broccoli had already been started earlier in April.

In early June the pepper growth begins to cover the black plastic pots, which are hidden by the beautiful foliage and by the salt-marsh hay mulch. The Swans buy hay each spring for its aesthetic appeal as well as for its moisture-retaining properties.

Key to achieving high yields of beautiful peppers, says John Swan, "is not to let the soil dry out, but to keep the plants growing vigorously by maintaining a constant supply of moisture, and by providing the right nutrients in the soil." Particularly for organic gardeners, timing is also critical. For those vegetables that are planted directly in the garden (lettuce, broccoli, Bok Choi, and so forth), the trick is to plant seeds as soon as possible after the soil warms up so that they can continue their growth before pests get big enough to do their damage. On the other hand, transplanting into the garden must be carefully timed so that the peppers and other young seedlings will not suffer early frost damage or have their growth interrupted by a spring cold snap. The Swans aim for a smooth and uninterrupted growth from the seeds started in March through the summer, when they begin an ongoing harvest that starts in August and continues through September. Some of their peppers become prizewinning specimens at the Pennsylvania Horticultural Society's annual Harvest Show, and others are lovingly prepared in Ann's ever-expanding repertoire of pepper dishes.

All
in the
Timing

HANNAH WISTER AND HER HUSBAND, William, moved their 18th-century house into the middle of a field at its present site in Oldwick, New Jersey, some 30 years ago. When she planned the 75-by-75-foot garden, Hannah had the hand-turned 18th-century finials copied from the cornice of the house and decoratively mounted on top of the fence posts. The colonial-inspired fence elegantly defines the garden and perhaps explains the reason for the lack of damage by the deer that ravage everything else outside the garden fence. "They seem to be a bit awed by the finials," Hannah says with a smile.

For the past 25 years the Wisters' gardener, Teo Gonzales, has lovingly and skillfully tended this formal New Jersey garden. The Wisters spend the height of the summer away from home, so Gonzales aims to produce most of the garden's vegetables for about June 15 and September 1, and to keep the garden neat and beautiful throughout the summer. The first planting takes place on St. Patrick's Day (March 17) and the second around the end of July, when the last beans have been harvested and the fall garden gets under way. Planting dates are, however, postponed if the soil is too cold to turn in the spring,

or if the rains come unseasonably in the middle of June, or if there are sudden heat waves or prolonged droughts. In the past few years, all of these climatic vagaries have reminded Teo that it is, after all, Mother Nature's garden and one must follow her schedule, not one's own. When the weather is erratic, he relies on his small solar greenhouse just outside the picket fence, where steps lead below ground to an area for starting and holding the cool-crop vegetables that are planted as near as possible to July 10. In early summer the greenhouse has an "instant garden" ready to be transplanted as soon as the spring garden has gone by. Here the vegetables are started that need more days to mature than those planted directly in the ground in early spring: parsnips (110 days), leeks (120 days), eggplant (110 days), and Brussels sprouts (125 days), to name a few. Forty tomato plants are begun here for a late rather than a midsummer harvest, to accommodate the Wisters' fall homecoming and for canning.

In the spring, along with four different kinds of lettuce, a sea of white English pea blossoms and their soft green tendrils occupies the first bed next to rows of deep green tender spinach and stalks of blue-green onions.

Above: *Eight wide rectangular beds, easily reached from both sides of the grassy paths, are pleasing to the eye as well as functional. In early spring, two of the earliest cool season vegetables are onions and spinach, offering contrasting textures and different shades of green. When the onion leaves turn yellow, gardener Teo Gonzales braids and bends them over to utilize the shade they provide for* young eggplant seedlings in the fall garden. Right: *Roses, both the standards placed within the garden and the luscious red climbers that hug the exterior of the picket fence, provide an ongoing decorative element in this New Jersey garden. Teo protects the less hardy rose varieties in winter by bending them over and covering them with salt hay at the first sign of frost.*

Above: *Since red currants—a relative of the gooseberry, which is also grown in the Wister garden—are little known to American gardeners, commercial availability is somewhat limited. Stark Brothers in Missouri offers the 'Red Lake' variety, and Raintree Nursery in Washington has both the Dutch variety 'Jhonkheer Van Tets' and the later-fruiting 'Red-Start' from England. (See Source List for addresses.)*

Borders of teucrium, sage, thyme, and lavender keep the carrots, beets, and radishes well defined, and the beautiful quiet symmetry of the vegetable beds only enhances the colorful display of the fence-hugging flowers that surround them—peonies, irises, roses, and a lively country bouquet of hollyhocks, delphiniums, and poppies in the mixed border at the back. In the middle are stone walks and a parterre centered on a sundial that came from the garden of Hannah's grandmother. It divides in half the four long north-south beds that are just wide enough to be reached from the grassy paths separating them. A long row of blossoming apple trees espaliered in the middle of the garden completes the spring garden picture.

The garden is just as charming in the fall, when crops of turnips, leeks, rutabagas, broccoli, cabbages, cauliflower, radicchio, Brussels sprouts, and parsnips—some of which are left for a sweetening by the first frost—are harvested. Also in fall, rich borders of zinnias, chrysanthemums, and dahlias replace the spring flowers as if by magic. In the Wister garden certain vegetables that don't fit strictly into Teo's early- or late-season schedule are allowed to straddle the seasons, providing a constant progression toward their final harvest. A few of these delicious additions are the ongoing beans, cucumbers, onions, raspberries, potatoes, tomatoes, and the chard that is cut and cut again throughout the summer and well into November.

Today Hannah Wister's tidy formal vegetable garden contains many of the same vegetables, flowers, and fruits that were brought to New Jersey by the first Dutch and Swedish settlers. Grown as standards or on trees, her red currant shrubs make a glorious display against the fence, a process that has taken seven years to get them to their present height of 5 feet. Hannah says, "Once you have them, they are very easy to propagate from cuttings and can be trained as espaliers or even cordons if you wish." Though currants can tolerate temperatures as low as −30 degrees, in the zone 6 Wister garden, where the average minimum temperature is −10 degrees, they, like their *Ribes* cousins the gooseberries and four roses trained as standards, are even more fragile than normal, and they require a winterizing protection against freezing. All the trunks are gently bent over and covered with salt hay at the first sign of frost.

Formal as the garden is, the element of experimentation is also present here—in 1995 Teo was proud of his first big bumper crop of several varieties of potatoes that he buried at the edge of his compost pile. And Hannah Wister plans to plant for the first time some 'Dr. Martin' lima beans, a modern version of the 18th-century equivalent found in many a vegetable garden when America was in its formative years two centuries ago.

CUCUMBERS

(Cucumis sativus)

All cucumbers (both for slicing and for pickling)—whether Asian, Middle Eastern, American, French, or other varieties—are considered fairly easy to grow in most home gardens throughout the country. They need 52–60 days to mature.

WHEN
Daytime temperatures should be consistently at least 60 degrees, and a minimum of 14 frost-free weeks of growing time is needed. Ideally, temperatures should be between 70 and 85 degrees.

WHERE
Plant in consistently moist soil, well composted with aged manure.

HOW
Sow seeds directly in the ground 4 inches apart and 1 inch deep, with 4 feet between the planting rows, 3–4 weeks after the last spring frost date. Alternatively, seeds can be started indoors (see page 170). Some cucumber growers prefer to plant their seeds in hills, like squash, 6 seeds to a hill set 5 feet apart. Germination, in all cases, should occur 6–10 days later. Thin to 2–3 seedlings per hill. If direct-seeded, thin to 6–8 inches apart by snipping off seedling tops, avoiding root disturbance of the remaining plants.

CARE
Until flowers have formed, feed plants a drink of fish emulsion every week. Provide trellises or tripods to support the cucumber vines, which may grow as tall as 6–8 feet. During summer's heat, water frequently to keep the fruit from becoming bitter and pithy. Harvest regularly to keep plants producing.

Growing an American Quilt

THE DESIGN OF PEGGY MCDONNELL'S 60-by-30-foot garden in Pepack, New Jersey, is that of an American patchwork quilt. Peggy herself is, in many ways, like those Colonial American quiltmakers, women who were both modest and reluctant to speak of their skills, yet determined and focused when it came to the perfection of their craft. With her husband, Murray, who died in 1991, Peggy raised nine children, who remember today in an almost reverential awe their mother's culinary ability: "I've never—*ever*—known anyone who could make as many meals from the garden for as long as she did," says her daughter Peggy Vance.

The layout of the garden has changed very little since the patchwork quilt idea first came into Peggy McDonnell's head. The blocks of her quilt—12 of them—are symmetrical, yet they are made up of different geometric shapes. Some squares are stitched together with salvia, and some blocks of vegetables are delineated by colorful narrow rows of flowers—zinnias, marigolds, dwarf snapdragons, dahlias—much as the squares of a quilt are often delineated by borders called "sashings" or "rails." The flowers are chosen to harmonize with the color and texture of the vegetables they border. The main sashing is a 3-foot-wide grassy path that runs north and south down the center. Two subsidiary grassy paths are flower-lined: one is gray and white and leads to the gazebo that looks out over a field of hops; the other is lined with multicolored flowers leading to a decoratively latticed toolshed.

The vegetables are rotated annually from square to square, in good vegetable gardening practice. Tomatoes are the exception—all 36 (15 different varieties) of them are planted in rows within their square, which, because of the plants' prominently tall, hand-hewn (by Peggy's gardening helper Joao Martins Pereira) cedar stakes, normally resembles a forest. Last year, however, Peggy whimsically formed arches of the indeterminate tomatoes that covered vines made of bittersweet.

Peggy's favorite time is in the early morning in early April, just after the compost and heavy rotted manure have been rototilled into the winter earth. "People have a mind-set that a garden is just the flowers, but I love what comes before just as much as the flowers and the vegetables in their prime. You must go back to the earth to see

Above: At the far end of the garden a "pot lady," fashioned after a Kenneth Turner design, stands knee deep in Swiss chard, offering a new humorous addition to the garden, much to the delight of Peggy's 21 grandchildren. The lady's hat—as baroque a creation as ever there was— brims over with magenta geraniums and transports this touch of color to new heights in the garden. Right: This nonclimbing lavender clematis is one of many blooms found in the multiflowered borders that serve as sashings for Peggy's American quilt garden. Overleaf, left. Bushels of tomatoes are harvested from the 15 varieties grown. Overleaf, right: Saint Fiacre, the patron saint of gardening, is surrounded by standard gooseberries in one of the squares of the quilt garden.

Above: *Lettuces forming triangles, trapezoids, and rectangles dominate the squares on both sides of the central path. The first on the left is centered by a copper rooster whose tail and coxcomb pick up the red- and bronze-tipped 'Lollo Rossa' lettuce leaves. In the next sections of the quilt garden, stitched together by a multiflowered border, are patches of carrots, leeks, and kale behind Saint Fiacre. On the other side of the path during the summer months, tomatoes, cabbages, beans, and eggplant all have their sections and are set off by flowers.*

the real beauty of a vegetable garden," Peggy observes.

"As early as possible in the early spring, we try to have our own fresh lettuce and get the lettuce blocks started by buying some lettuce plants of different varieties. These tide us over until our own seeds ordered from catalogs have started to produce." Lettuce blocks are 12-foot squares slashed with two diagonal rows of beets that

create three interlocking isosceles triangles on each side of the path. Functional yet beautiful bluestone pavers make harvesting the lettuce easier and offer yet another color and texture to the color-balanced rows of red- and green-leafed lettuces. Most of the lettuce seeds are from Shepherd's Garden Seeds: looseleaf varieties—both green and 'Red Oakleaf' and 'Lollo Rossa'—and contrasting formal rosettes from the bibb/limestone collection, including 'Merveille des Quatre Saisons'. Both the colors and textures of the larger crispy romaines 'Rouge d'Hiver' and 'Romance' contrast effectively with the curly leaves of 'Très Fine Endive'. All the lettuce rows lead to a centered square of purple chives surrounding a stunning copper rooster, one of the last presents Peggy's husband, Murray, gave her before he died.

Different stages of growth in the lettuces, from 2-inch seedlings to full lush heads, create an effect like the raised appliqués of 19th-century quilts. On another level textural contrasts are achieved through a variety of accessories. Tall, dark green wooden obelisks provide support for clean white sweet peas in spring, and architectural features, such as the two wrought-iron-embellished wooden gates, the latticed gazebo, and the toolhouse, are all festooned with climbing roses or purple or pink clematis.

Even the marking tags are beautiful—oval, flat pieces of baked clay glued to a heavy nail and then stuck in the ground hold hand-scripted names of the vegetables, a decorative as well as practical touch for keeping seedlings identified. Occasionally, like a scrap of velvet pieced into a quilt just because it was so fine, a showy flower might occupy a square—an exquisite new chocolate cosmos (*Cosmos atrosanguineus*), for example.

Peggy remembers her own mother's garden and the bountiful display of flowers and vegetables. "For as long as I can remember we always had a garden. Flowers were everywhere—in the vegetable garden to be sure." In the next generation Pia, Peggy's oldest daughter, says, "I'm not at the gardening level of my mother, but I love it and some of us definitely got that from her. It is a matter of the same values: liking to grow things, being proud of what you grow, and liking to eat what you grow."

LETTUCE

(Lactuca sativa)

The main requirements for beautiful heads of leafy lettuce are a good, composted soil; plenty of consistent moisture; and an even, cool temperature. Plants mature in 50–60 days.

WHEN
For an ongoing harvest, plant every 2 weeks from early spring until early summer, as consistently hot weather causes bolting. Sow again in late summer for a fall harvest before frost. In mild-winter zones, lettuce can be planted most of the year.

WHERE
Healthy, tender lettuce grows best in soil that is moist but not soggy. Many of the cut-and-come-again, or nonheading, varieties can be broadcasted evenly over a well-cultivated, weed-free bed.

HOW
Direct-sow seeds and then thin plants to 12 inches apart in rows or wide beds as soon as soil temperatures rise to between 60 and 80 degrees. Cover the seeds with ¼ inch of fine soil, potting mix, or compost; tamp down lightly and water with a gentle spray.

CARE
Lettuce thinnings, as seedlings grow to 3–5 inches, make a delicious salad straight from the garden. Harvest by cutting back with scissors to 2 inches above soil level.

Soul Garden
in the
City

IN INNER-CITY PHILADELPHIA, IN THE HEART of old Germantown, Amos T. Rogers tends a garden that for nine years took first prize at the Philadelphia Horticultural Society's City Gardeners' Contest. Besides the 100 pots and baskets of flowers hanging from the fences and trees, portulaca, snapdragons, and other colorful bedding plants are scattered here and there to enhance the beauty of the vegetables, just the way his grandparents taught him when he was growing up in Knightdale, 10 miles outside of Raleigh, North Carolina. "I had a part to play just like the adults did," he says. "I learned how to garden from them and it was a way of being with them." Indeed, one recognizes the Rogers home in Germantown by the flower-lined walkway and bright red salvia in the front yard just the way "at my grandmother's and my Aunt Mary's, you could always tell who lived in the house because of the flowers by the front door. They were called the 'flower ladies.'"

The vegetable garden is not visible from the street, so the sight of the entire city-lot garden growing in healthy abundance around the side of the house almost takes your breath away.

When the city tore down the building on the lot next to Amos's house in 1980, he bought the lot and, single-handedly, began to clean up and transform the narrow 74-foot by 200-foot area into the beautiful garden it is today. He worked before and after his regular job as a forklift operator, "as early and as late as you could see. I removed tons of pipes and construction material and had to go over the soil twice to remove all the stones. Since the city didn't bring in any topsoil when they removed the house, I have been adding mushroom topsoil, aged manure, and compost every year. Mine is new soil every year, so there's no need to rotate the vegetables." Every fall Amos tills in the "new earth" by hand and levels it with a heavy rake, so that 50 percent of the work is already done and he doesn't "get discouraged with too much left to do in the spring."

Amos Rogers is very much aware of the design of his garden. Aside from his decorative curving borders and the contrast of foliage and color combinations, he forms both the vertical and horizontal rows with the concern of an artist, "because it makes it look nicer and more like a farm in the country. Everyone likes the country garden

Above: *Summer squash and eggplant blossoms show among the purple cabbages and kale in Amos T. Rogers's city-lot garden in the old Germantown section of Philadelphia. By midsummer the cucumber vines in the background are well on their way up the chain-link fence. Right: Amos sits under his pear tree in the Adirondack chair he made himself, reflecting: "You see, my grandparents raised me and I began as a kid. That's all they knew about—gardening and farming in North Carolina. I didn't throw away all the ideas. I just revived them in a new setting, and you see what's happening."*

look in the city." Although he never draws a plan on paper, his design has a clear sense of symmetry. He studies photographs from the previous summer to see how to improve the garden design.

The first vegetables planted in the spring are the onions—usually during the third week in March. Because his timing is intuitive rather than calendar-bound, Amos Rogers's planting schedule is nearly foolproof. "A lot of what I do just comes naturally," he admits. "I can't explain it. Like the farmers, I just know it's time to plant." Next, the white potatoes go in fairly early, during the last week in March because they grow as tubers below the ground, and can stand the cold. "Sweet potatoes and yams take a long time to grow and need a warmer soil. I start them indoors in the boiler room from small potatoes, then move them outdoors to the cold frames, and by the time they are ready to move into the garden, they have developed into healthy plants."

If it is warm enough by April, he begins planting the bush and pole varieties of string beans in different parts of the garden for continuous harvesting beginning six weeks later. Usually, however, it is the first week in May. "The first planting is in four rows, then three rows two weeks later, and finally two rows two or three weeks later. After they are picked I continue to replace all the rows, right up until the second week in August."

The real staples of this garden, however, are traditionally southern: black-eyed peas, lima beans, cabbages, yams, and collard greens. They are all started in the cold frames and are not transplanted out in the garden until

Left: *Amos takes full advantage of a chain-link fence that borders his city-lot garden. Cucumbers are given ample space to spread and grow vertically in full sun.*

OKRA

(Abelmoschus esculentus)

There are no secrets for growing this warm-season, tropical vegetable, which takes 52–60 days from seed to the first edible pod (best eaten when 3–4 inches long). Even though it is America's least popular vegetable, according to the U.S. Department of Agriculture, okra lovers enjoy it fresh from the garden, steamed briefly, then seasoned with butter, salt, and pepper.

WHEN
Direct-seed as soon as the soil reaches 68 degrees (as Amos Rogers does). Plant a second crop in June in the warmer southern and western zones.

WHERE
Grow in full sun and in areas where summers are consistently hot. The soil should be well drained and composted.

HOW
Sow seeds ¾ inch deep directly in the ground. Thin to 18 inches apart when the plants are 2 inches tall (set dwarf varieties 12 inches apart). In short-season regions, start seedlings indoors in pots and transplant when the soil is warm enough.

CARE
Continuously harvest plants—do not allow to fully ripen or the plants will stop producing and the okra will become fibrous and tough.

Above: *Curving paths connect the three main sections of the garden, created by Amos Rogers in 1970 from a vacant lot next to his house. The pear tree in the center was the only tree on the 74-by-200-foot city lot. The vegetables and flowers are arranged according to contrasting textures and colors for a pleasing design, and Amos has* added *cherry, apple, and apricot trees for a cool place from which to admire the garden.* Right: *In addition to his favorite 'Golden Bell' peppers, Amos grows these 'California Wonder' peppers next to his 'Blue Curled Vates' kale.*

May, after the soil is considerably warmer. At that time rows of okra, another essential vegetable in this garden, are planted directly in the ground and later thinned. At least half the seeds are saved over from year to year, but some come from southern seed companies that Amos has learned he can count on (see pages 183–84).

The four rows of black-eyed peas, or field peas, grow happily next to 'Blue Lake' string beans and bush limas. All are handsomely set off by a square border of gray-green Savoy cabbage, and an occasional dot of purple cabbage turns up randomly "just because it looks pretty there." Black-eyed peas are easy to grow. Amos says one can simply plant some of the dried "store-bought" ones that come in a package at the grocery store because they do just as well.

Like okra and black-eyed peas, collards, or "collie greens" as they are sometimes affectionately called, are "soul food" mainstays. A member of the brassica family, collards are rich in vitamin A and low in calories, and contain a wealth of minerals, such as potassium, calcium, iron, and zinc. After most other vegetables have been turned under, even after the first frost, Brussels sprouts, turnips, kale, and mustard greens are still to be picked, but collard greens stay until the end and are still found fresh in the Rogers kitchen at Christmastime.

Passersby on Walnut Lane sometimes smell the collard greens that Rena Rogers cooks in bacon drippings, along with the black-eyed peas slowly simmered with hamhock, the unforgettable aroma of baked sweet potato pies, or the okra fried or stewed with tomatoes and baby limas all fresh from the garden.

Many of the more fragile, heat-loving vegetables such as eggplant, green and yellow peppers, cucumbers, and the 60 tomato plants have also been started in the cold frame and are moved out in early June. Peppers are often planted at the base of the tomatoes so that later in the season, when the tomato leaves start yellowing, the peppers are tall enough to hide the unsightly bases and help to keep the garden looking as pretty as Amos insists that it be. Amos's favorite yellow pepper, the 'Golden Bell' variety from Harris Seeds (see Source List), is handsomely interplanted in a celery border that follows the winding path and wraps around the gentle curve of the garden. In early summer the soft yellow hibiscus-like blossoms of the okra plants dominate the large area of the garden in front of the 6-foot-tall fruit-laden tomato towers and add immeasurably to the garden's beauty.

"Watermelons, like yams and sweet potatoes, take longer to mature than any other vegetable in Pennsylvania (at least in our zone 6) and they all love the heat." In the Rogers garden the watermelon and honeydew melon vines are sometimes allowed to trail underfoot in order to capture the heat from the stone walkways and ripen to perfection.

Finally, fruit trees, including cherry, peach, and plum, have been added to the pear tree that was the only tree on the lot when they bought it in 1980. Rena Rogers freezes any fruit not eaten from the trees for their winter use, along with the blackberries, grapes, and strawberries that also grow in the garden.

Amos Rogers, sitting under the pear tree in his home-made blue Adirondack chair, admits that he is blessed. Looking out over his garden admiring his vegetables and the trees laden with fruit, he offers philosophically, "There is more than one side to life. This is the best side. You get the other side anyway, but this is the nice side where you get all the live things, doing God's work."

A Balance of Paradoxes

ANYONE WHO WRITES ABOUT RYAN GAINEY'S garden in Decatur, Georgia, begins by describing the owner himself—his charming eccentricities, his whimsicality, his unique and often contradictory personality, or even his flamboyant clothing style. The way he speaks, like his clothes and his garden, simply reflects the man himself—much as Ryan believes that all gardens should reflect their owners. And this garden in particular reveals a man of paradoxes.

There are quiet, romantic places for the nurturing of the soul and elsewhere dramatic statements of vibrant color. "But," says Ms. Sam Flowers, a garden-designer friend of Ryan's from Dothan, Alabama, "Ryan's gardens are never excessive. He knows when to quit." His vegetable garden reflects restraint: he grows only enough vegetables to supply his own table and only those he likes to eat and can grow well. In the same seemingly paradoxical vein, the garden offers the illusion of being spontaneously planted with luxurious abandon, but a strong sense of order prevails. Finally, some ordinary southern natives are combined with exotic specimens rarely seen. One marvels at how well thought out the combinations of plants are, a feat that could be achieved only by an experienced plantsman.

Ryan Gainey's three-lot city garden formerly belonged to a family of commercial flower growers whose six greenhouses were functional but, as always with old greenhouses, in need of repair when he bought the property in 1982. Three of the greenhouses built in the 1930s have been taken down to make room for separate gardens. Of the three that remain, one is used, conventionally, for plant propagation. Another, the "Conservatory," has primarily a more unconventional use. It is conveniently near the back door and serves as "the shower room," as well as a dovecote for his white pigeons and a magnificent foil for the 'Mermaid' rose that climbs happily over the top.

The last of the existing greenhouses is the "Dugout," half in the ground. Ryan explains its nonhorticultural use with his typical quick wit: "It's a place to drink champagne and eat poke salad when the tornadoes are coming." (Poke greens, according to Ryan, are any kind of southern greens five times boiled.) When not doubling as a prestorm shelter, the Dugout serves as a cold frame for

Above: *Ryan Gainey's art as floral designer shows clearly in his own garden, where he plays with contrasts, paradoxes, and color. Purple and chartreuse is one of the repeating color combinations in his Georgia garden, such as the luscious juxtaposition of purple-flecked buttercrunch lettuce and vibrant purple cabbages. Right: Ryan believes that beauty for the soul and nourishment for the body* are equally important. *A vegetable garden should have both. Following pages, left: The pea family (Pisum sativum)* convenes: *flat snow peas, new sugar snaps, and fat old-fashioned shelling peas, surrounded by scented sweet pea blossoms. Right: Lemon and golden thyme creep onto the paths outlining the diamond beds.*

Above: *In a French* potager *this would be called* fraise de bois, *but in the United States the native American is known as the alpine strawberry (Fragaria vesca) and is just as delicious. The small, sweet fruits look particularly inviting in gold or red (available from Thompson & Morgan) as they spill over some of the beds edging Ryan's vegetable garden.*

holding some of the numerous flowering plants and vegetables that are tried and often make their way into his botanical paradise. One of the latest Ryan is looking forward to testing is a pole bean called 'Tennessee Greasybacks' sent to him by a friend who knew how he would delight in the humor of its name.

The axial design of the rectangular vegetable garden is strong: three turreted diamond-shaped beds outlined in Korean boxwood 'Winter Gem' placed tip to tip with a 'Fairy' standard rose in the center of each, and progressive plantings of basil at their feet. Starkly unpretentious

concrete slabs from the former greenhouses form the steppingstones through the garden.

In its more abundant season, parsley is allowed to form flower heads—as beautiful as Queen Anne's lace—that will eventually find their way into some of Ryan Gainey's more lavish floral creations at one of his Atlanta businesses, The Cottage Garden, which specializes in spectacular flower arrangements for the Atlanta social scene. In his garden, the parsley and other vegetables are allowed to respond to their own "horticultural architecture," to soften the hard edges of the geometric design by spilling out into the golden thyme-lined paths.

The size of the vegetable garden, 35 feet by 25 feet, was dictated by the dimensions of the first of the former greenhouses to be torn down. Ryan took advantage of the brick greenhouse walls, which look much older than their 1930s vintage, adding immeasurably to the vegetable garden and giving it a romantic Old World look. The brick walls together with the trellises of red cedar (*Juniperus virginiana*) that Ryan has mounted on top of them form the architectural structure of the garden and provide a 9-foot-high rectangular framework for the climbers—roses, clematis, and, later, tomatoes—during the summer. In the winter, a dramatic mosaic is created by the combination of the old brick walls, the stepping-stones, the rustic trellises, the patterning of the boxwood diamonds, and the accompanying triangular beds along the wall—together with (when the temperature doesn't fall too low) patterns of arugula, flat-leafed parsley, and kale.

Through the seasons each area of the garden has its own contrasts of textures and patterns. Equally important in this garden are the harmonies of color. In May the roses begin to bloom on the vegetable garden wall ('Goldfinch', 'Fortune's Double Yellow', climbing 'Cécile Brünner', and 'Silver Moon'), carefully chosen to slightly overlap their flowering schedules. Also in early May the evergreen Japanese hydrangea vine, *Schizophragma hydrangeoides* 'Moonlight', is in full bloom, and near it when its blooms have gone by, the trellises will be covered with the green peas and sugar snaps whose light green foliage is the essence of spring. In addition to the

Right: Diamonds are everywhere in Ryan Gainey's garden, on the trellis above a former greenhouse's old brick foundation, as boxwood dividers for his vegetable beds, and as zigs and zags through the garden paths.

triangular broccoli beds next to the wall are other triangular beds edged with alpine strawberries—yellow pineapple-scented ones as well as the delicious bright red variety. As the season progresses, the 'Ruby Red' chard demands attention, eclipsing the lettuces, and even later 'Supersweet 100' tomatoes tumble over the trellises nestling into the foliage of the evergreen hydrangea vine. In the fall a second crop of kale arrives, which continues into winter, along with the arugula, flat-leafed parsley, and whatever cool-season vegetables strike Ryan's fancy.

Ryan does not consider the soil a particular challenge; it can be improved. But the 100-degree temperatures that come suddenly and often to Decatur from May to September sometimes mean he has to abandon his vegetable garden, and restore it when the weather cools down. Extending the seasons is his most fascinating challenge. "People down here go to sleep in the fall like their gardens do, I guess. Gardens are not just for one spring blooming season or for a few days. I try in this garden to show the beauty of the plants during their complete growing cycle: their hips, their fall foliage, their buds, and their seedpods as well as their blooms. In September we have tea olives (*Osmanthus fragrans*) and then comes the wintersweet (*Chimonanthus praecox*) with its delicious winter fragrance. And then the camellias start and go right up until spring. In reality a good garden is eternal spring—not in terms of a season but eternally springing forth and bringing you something. Gardens are the best reflection of man's history, his taste and style, and also in the past they were a good marker of the peaceful times when man could afford to turn to his own pleasure—the garden."

Left: Rustic trellises made of eastern red cedar lift the garden higher into the sunlight. Once the young peas (sweet, sugar snap, or English) have gone by, tomatoes or clematis climb to their places to cover the trellis, which is never without tendrils of one kind or another.

SNOW PEAS

Snow Pea, Sugar or Chinese Pea, or Snap Pea
(Pisum sativum)

Both snow and the newer snap peas grow on the bush or on the vine. Plants mature in 60–65 days.

WHEN
In mild-winter areas, plant from October through February; air temperature should be 60–75 degrees. Ryan Gainey plants snap peas with tiny *petits pois* in mid-February; after 6 weeks the plants flower, and he harvests 60 days later.

WHERE
Soil should be slightly "sweetened" with bonemeal or lime at planting time (no additional fertilizing is necessary). Plant vining varieties next to a sturdy 8-foot trellis; bush plants need supports, too, for tendrils to wrap around.

HOW
Sow seeds 1 inch deep and 1 inch apart. Thin to 2 inches apart. Plant in several short rows or 3-inch parallel bands rather than in a long single row.

CARE
Avoid overhead watering, which causes mildew. Apply mulch midseason to hold in moisture, to keep soil temperature down as the weather warms up, and to enrich the soil.

Eighteenth-Century Moravian Know-how

THE 18TH CENTURY IS ALIVE AND WELL AT Old Salem, North Carolina—and in certain vegetable patches the early 19th century too! The well-tended gardens, the shops and homes in this restored Moravian Church community give the public an idea of life as it was before the town ceased to function as a religious community in the mid-19th century. Today the restored vegetable gardens are a strong reminder of how much gardens meant as earthly paradises and as practical necessities.

The hardworking, music-loving Protestant sect is one of the oldest, dating back to 1457, with roots in the Czech reformation and closely linked to Lutheranism. Known as the Bohemian Brethren, they first came to America in 1735, settling in Savannah, Georgia. Ten years before the American Revolution, a small group of Moravians from Pennsylvania purchased a 100,000-acre tract to be called Wachovia in the idyllic wooded hills of Piedmont, North Carolina.

Salem became the center of the tract of Wachovia and was known for its crafts and "honest and hardworking tradespeople," not as an agricultural community. Yet the gardens were a necessity in Old Salem, providing what was consumed by each household and a few flowers for their aesthetic enjoyment.

At Salem the Church owned and leased lots, each identical in size, to individuals, who built right on the street, with a courtyard behind the house for a children's play yard, washtubs, chickens, bake ovens, woodsheds, and general household activities. Beyond the yard was the "family garden," laid out in rectangular plots or "squares," in the European Renaissance style prevalent at the time. There were usually six or eight plots on a central axis that divided the squares equally in a north-south direction with wide grassy paths in between. Julianne Berckman, former horticulturist at Old Salem, points out that this system of wide beds and the elimination of paths along straight rows of vegetables yields as much as 50 percent more planting space.

Today as then, visitors enjoy the peaceful atmosphere of Old Salem. Hollyhocks, daffodils, love-in-a-mist, tall stalks of delphinium, and bachelor's buttons are tucked in between the fruit trees or at the corners of the vegetable beds. All the vegetables and flowers have been

Above: *Kohlrabi and comfrey* (Symphytum officinale), *a medicinal herb usually found in 18th-century "family gardens" such as the Triebel garden at Old Salem, the reconstructed Moravian village in Winston-Salem,* *North Carolina.* Right: *At Old Salem, cherry trees remind us of how highly prized they were in 18th-century American gardens.*

Left: *The historic restoration of Old Salem gardens began in 1972. Visitors today will see the gardens re-created as they were in the 18th century, when the Moravian church owned the property and leased it to families who tended the gardens as their own.*

Right: *Kohlrabi is an underground member of the cabbage family whose bulb-stems have traditionally been a delicacy in Northern European countries and was a staple in the Czech-American Moravian community of Old Salem. It, like most other cabbages, is planted as a cool-season vegetable.*

carefully chosen from plant lists available in the Old Salem archives to represent the original planting plan. In this Germanic community, root vegetables such as kohlrabi, turnips, parsnips, and salsify predominate. Salsify (*Tragopogon porrifolius*) was confused then, as it is today, with another vegetable known as black salsify or black oyster plant (*Scorzonera hispanica*).

The re-creation of the Old Salem gardens began in 1972 and was based on archaeology and on church records, 18th-century plant lists, and diaries in the archives. The gardens, together with the different styles of fences and other architectural elements of the 18th and 19th centuries, have been re-created as authentically as possible to resemble those under the scrutiny of the Moravian Church brethren in the 18th and 19th centuries. Director of horticulture Darrell Spencer oversees the ongoing re-creation of the gardens. "Summer comes early in the South. I generally think of our spring season as pretty much ending come the first of June," Darrell explains. "By the second week in June it's getting hot. And we have a particular challenge here in Winston-Salem since many of our Old World plants—and we have more than a hundred heirloom varieties, including the 'Sandwich Island Mammoth' salsify (pre-1900), 'Early Purple Vienna' kohlrabi (pre-1860), and 'Lazy Wife' pole beans (1810)—don't react favorably to ninety-degree days end on end. And the other big challenge is that we have to keep things going for the visiting public." Old Salem takes pride in offering three seasonal gardens: the spring, summer, and, most impressive of all, the fall garden that continues until Thanksgiving and in a good year until Christmas. Fall gardens are particularly challenging because these are cool weather crops that must be established during the hottest two weeks of the year, at the end of August.

SALSIFY

Salsify *(Tragopogon porrifolius)* and Scorzonera or Black Salsify *(Scorzonera hispanica)*

Eighteenth-century gardeners such as Thomas Jefferson grew these cool-season vegetables, but today they are not common. Both are white fleshed, grow similar to parsnips (see page 45), and can take as long as 150 days to mature.

WHEN

Soak seeds overnight and sow directly as soon as the soil can be worked. In mild climates, plant a second crop in early fall to mature by early spring.

WHERE

Slightly acidic to neutral soil (pH 6.5–7.0) that receives full sun is best, although plants tolerate both shade and various types of soil in all zones.

HOW

Plant (as is done at Old Salem) in deeply cultivated, enriched soil in blocks (12 seeds per square foot), or sow seeds directly in the ground 2 inches apart, ¼–½ inch deep, in rows 1 foot apart, covering with ¼ inch soil. Thin salsify to 4–6 inches apart when 2 sets of leaves appear; leave 1 foot between scorzonera.

CARE

Soil well composted at planting time needs no additional fertilizer. Plant with radishes to help identify rows of seeds, which are often confused with grasslike weeds.

3

the

M I D W E S T

*"When you stand upon a high place over-looking the prairie, what seems to you its deepest meaning?
Some say the dominant note is peacefulness—that this middlewestern country will never be invaded by
a foreign foe, and the landscape expresses this sense of security."*

WILHELM MILLER, *THE PRAIRIE SPIRIT IN LANDSCAPE GARDENING,* 1915

Lessons of the Prairie

When Wilhelm Miller outlined the characteristics of the "Prairie Style" in 1915, he, and his fellow members of the Prairie School movement, Frank Lloyd Wright and Jens Jensen, praised the natural beauty of the midwestern prairie as being uniquely American. Not only did Miller advocate a complete disassociation from European garden models, he also cited the importance of native plants. Both Miller and Jensen stressed the conservation of endangered species—wildflowers and native grasses in particular—and a repetition of the horizontal line that symbolizes the prairie itself.

As Americans become more conscious of their own garden heritage—not to mention the unique natural history of North America—more midwestern gardeners are seeking out plants and garden styles that epitomize the ideals of the Prairie School.

For some of these gardeners, the unbroken horizons of the prairie offer an opportunity to create a garden that seems to stretch from sea to shining sea—or at least from the house to the cornfield beyond. For others, the influence of America's agricultural tradition flavors the choice of garden vegetables and the striking simplicity of garden design.

Inspired by Monticello

RON AND JULIA RICHARDS'S GARDEN, IN Edinburgh, Indiana, is a large cocreative endeavor covering 9 acres. One-half of their "outdoor living space" is a wooded area where Solomon's seal, blackberry lilies (*Belamcanda chinensis*), wild larkspur and phlox, narcissus, and violets have been naturalized over the years. The couple divides the gardening responsibilities; but the labor is shared and, more often than not, is done side by side. Julia Richards says, "We garden because we love the process. When we get tired and take a Sunday afternoon off, it isn't long before one of us is saying, 'If we start home now, we will still have two hours of daylight left to garden.' We take our lunch or supper to a garden bench to eat. We take our guests to the garden to visit. The garden is where we work and where we rest." As with many treasured things in life, Ron and Julia have been able to pass on the love of this special garden to their children as well as the more tangible fruits of their labor, which are shared with neighbors, extended family, and their employees at their grain elevator.

Weddings and important family celebrations involving several generations have been tied to the garden.

Their daughter, Dana, was married in the garden several years ago, and recently their son, Andy, and his fiancée wanted their wedding at a time when the garden was full of flowers and the wedding guests could look out at the garden at its peak. The date of the wedding also had to coincide with the timing of the harvesting of the corn at its perfect moment so that guests could share the family's legendary homegrown corn-on-the-cob. "We have reared a couple of garden foodaholics," Julia admits.

Preparations for another wedding celebration, Julia's parents' 50th anniversary in 1985, initiated the vegetable garden's major expansion and started it seriously on its way to becoming the 1-acre garden it is today. After that anniversary party, the garden continued to grow for the next five years as one or more gardens or garden buildings were added each season. "Our lives were garden-centered. At one point, Ron said I was going at it like I was killing snakes," Julia laughs.

"Ron and I have always had a vegetable garden or had access to our parents' gardens." This was true even when they were teachers—Ron of biology and Julia of English—before they started their own business and

Above: *Julia Richards offers an unconventional approach in the design of her garden. Instead of letting the foliage take a secondary role as a filler to enhance her flowers, the strongly decorative blue-green kale is* a bold focal point, set off and framed by splashes of colorful zinnias, marigold, and cosmos. Right: Ron and Julia Richards of Edinburgh, Indiana, with their most frequently used machine, the tiller.

began gardening together, near Edinburgh on the rural property once farmed by Julia's grandfather. As with Julia's parents and grandparents, all born and raised in Bartholomew County, for Ron and Julia gardening is a way of life they wouldn't be without. Julia's great-grand-parents came from Germany and Ireland in the 1840s. They followed the Ohio River up to southern Indiana, began farming there, and never left. Ron's family, also immigrants three generations ago, lived in the neighboring county of Johnson, where Ron was born and perhaps inherited, through his Scottish forefathers, a love of Scotch kale, one of the couple's best-grown vegetables.

Ron and Julia appreciate the beauty of the horizontal lines and the vastness of their natural midwestern scene. They took advantage of the large, flat space bordered today on the north by a forest of tall, slim walnut and Kentucky coffee trees. At the forest's edge the area has been cleared and planted with grass. Picnic tables and resting spots in the shade tempt visitors to bide their time while enjoying the long horizontal view through the trees out onto the open cornfields extending far into the horizon. Another broad field of corn defines the garden's southern parameters. The large rectangular gardens sit in the otherwise open space, planted with alternating rows of vegetables, flowers, and herbs. Ron built the few simple structures on the property, including a toolshed, a barn, and a reassembled smokehouse that had belonged to Julia's grandfather. All add a feeling of age and permanence to what is basically a fairly new garden.

The inspiration for the design came from the vegetable garden at Monticello, which Julia admires. "When we stood looking out over the garden at Monticello, and I

Left: The fields of corn framing the southern side of this Indiana garden invite the spectator into the seemingly infinite horizontality of the midwestern landscape, a symbol of tranquillity and the essence of American landscape design.

KALE & COLLARDS

Kale and Collards *(Brassica oleracea,* Acephala group*)*, and Mustard Greens *(B. juncea)*

Increasingly popular in the American diet because of their high content of cancer-fighting carotenoids and vitamins and their low caloric count, kale and collards, nonheading members of the cabbage family, are particularly well known in southern states. Mustard greens are also becoming more popular for the same reasons, both the Asian varieties and the American ones widely grown in the South, where for centuries they traditionally have been boiled or steamed simply as "greens" and served as an accompaniment to corn bread and black-eyed peas. Plants generally mature in 48–60 days.

WHEN
Start seeds in very early spring, or in midsummer in the North or in late summer in southern and coastal areas for a fall harvest.

WHERE
Plant in full sun in soil enriched with aged manure.

HOW
Start in flats and transplant seedlings ½ inch deep and 1 inch apart once 2 sets of leaves have developed. Thin plants to 12–18 inches apart.

CARE
Most greens respond to a well-composted, fertile soil, rich in nitrogen. Keep well weeded and moist for continued leaf production.

made noises of appreciation and excitement, Ron asked me to remember that Jefferson had 250 slaves, thereby suggesting that I lower my expectations." Nevertheless, the shape of Jefferson's long garden stayed with them, as did its wide grassy paths. In the garden such paths offer convenient access across the three 30-foot-wide plots next to their long garden. One of the two other sections, or "add-ons," to the main garden is dedicated to geometrically arranged herb and flower beds. The other is a large plot called the north garden at the far end for those vegetables that do not fit into the main garden. Benches and bluebird houses made and distributed by Ron for the preservation of the endangered bluebird are strategically placed to reinforce the feeling of leisure and simple natural pleasures in the garden.

Each year Julia designs the garden in her head rather than drawing it out on paper. She rotates most of the vegetables, tries a few new ones, and occasionally eliminates those that didn't do particularly well, giving a feeling of spontaneity to the garden design. She is always on the lookout for unusual flowers that are not often seen in vegetable gardens, adding a new twist to the evenly spaced straight rows of vegetables. A startling bouquet of godetia may appear at the end of a row of beans, or a row of gladioli or blue ageratum may alternate with rows of beets and turnips.

In the spring Ron can till the compost into the entire garden in an hour thanks to their rototiller and the exceptionally wide rows. Recently they have begun to add, at the same time as the spring composting, processed chicken manure, which they prefer to regular steer manure because the numbers are low.

Next, steel rods wound with string are laid down to mark the rows, and the planting is usually done all in one day. "Ron makes the furrow with the hoe handle and I'm the seed sprinkler, then Ron comes back and tamps down the earth over the seeds." The rows are rototilled throughout the season, eliminating most of the weeds and aerating the soil as well as eliminating some of the fungi and insects that could plague the garden.

About 40 tomato plants are started in the greenhouse, then moved to cages in one of the add-on sections of the garden, along with zucchini and yellow squash, potatoes, and the other vegetables and flowers that failed to fit into the main "Monticello-inspired" rectangular garden or its neighboring plots. Eventually Julia's parents will can over 60 quarts of tomatoes for the family's winter larders. Zucchini, cucumbers, eggplant, cabbage, and peppers are usually also started in mid-March in the greenhouse. Most of the kale, however, is direct-seeded in April—including the 'Red Russian', the dark curly 'Verdura' originally from Holland, and the Italian heirloom 'Lacinato', all from Shepherd's Garden Seeds (see Source List). Their rows of 'Vates Dwarf Blue Curled Scotch', a variety originally from Scotland (ordered from Seeds Blum; see page 183), where the greatest kale eaters come from, are spectacular to look at.

Recently a kale relative in the brassica family, mustard greens, has been given a special patch in the garden just to self-sow on its own, one of the things Julia learned from her grandmother's garden. "We collect books about gardening to read in the winter, and we do learn from them. But some of the best learning takes place when we talk to experienced gardeners and other like-minded people.

Preceding pages: *Seen through the rows of blue kale, cosmos, and beanpoles, the smokehouse that once belonged to Julia's grandfather adds a nostalgic note. Though this one is now used primarily as a garden storage shed, smokehouses were a common part of the midwestern scene in the late 19th century.*

Left: *Julia and Ron Richards are active participants in the annual county fair, where their vegetable garden produce—any of which makes a decorative display—is apt to take first prize.*

Right: *Hardy ageratum (Eupatorium coelestinum) frames and enlivens the herb garden that includes summer savory, basil, and cilantro, Julia's favorite herbs.*

Little
Experiment
on the Prairie

WHEN DICK AND MARCIA MUSSMAN MOVED from Indianapolis to rural central Indiana in 1970, they wanted a very different life from the one they had led in the city—a country life that would be as independent as they could manage. At that time Marcia, a talented weaver, had never tended sheep, spun wool, or grown the plants to make her own dye. All of these tasks and the tending of an ever-changing garden have become a part of Marcia Mussman's daily life.

"I was drawn to this particular property because of the pasture—Jens Jensen and Frank Lloyd Wright might call it a prairie—and woods, and the stream that meanders all the way through it. This is not what a typical farmer who plants corn, soybeans, and wheat would look for in land, but it is perfect for cows and sheep and it abounds with wildlife and birds."

The transformation in 1988 from an ordinary row-upon-row vegetable garden, which Marcia had tended for the first few years, into a beautiful one did not so much involve changing the choice of vegetables themselves; rather, it meant a complete overhauling of the bones—that is, a redefinition of the space and the addition of a garden accessory that would tie the whole design together. Even though Marcia's annual experimentation in the planting and her good vegetable gardening practice of crop rotation bring a few changes to the garden each year, the paths and the parameters stay the same.

The open sunny area, where the ordinary vegetable garden had been, was still the logical place for the new garden, because it was the only space near the house that was not shaded by pine, spruce, oak, and maple trees. In order to emphasize the contrast between the modest 56-by-90-foot vegetable garden and its setting, John Esterline, a prominent Indianapolis landscape architect, designed for the Mussmans a formal garden with a circle of 'Simplicity' roses at its center. He gave it a monumental touch by placing an antique terra-cotta oil jar at the very center of the circle. "We chose 'Simplicity' because it is supposed to be very hardy and disease resistant, but I did have to replace six or eight of them a few years after we had planted them," Marcia warns.

The garden is bound on one side by a row of asparagus, whose light green, feathery foliage softly delineates the entire western length of the garden. A long row of

Above: A 1930s barn emphasizes the rural character of the landscape. A glimpse beyond the walnut and pine trees lining the property brings the prairie feeling right up to the front door.
Right: Marcia Mussman believes tomatoes in Indiana "definitely have a different taste from those in other parts of the country—because of the soil and weather conditions, and the varieties are different here too."

Left: *Marcia Mussman's experiment on the prairie involves tending her sheep and gathering and dying their wool.* Above: *By the time the vegetables are in their most productive stage in July, the garden loses some of its formality. However, one of the four wooden bean tepees supports the hyacinth beans and decoratively towers above exuberant patches of basil and squash.*

strawberries parallel to flowers grown for dyeing (tansy, madder, chamomile, yarrow, and weld) defines the eastern border. Four decorative wooden towers at each corner of the garden support the purple tendrils of hyacinth beans and Malabar spinach and add to the symmetry. They also provide another dimension to this essentially flat area.

Although the garden has a formal plan, the vistas in between the blocks of sweet corn and tomatoes at the far end of the garden invite the spectator into the cornfields beyond. An important characteristic of the Prairie Style, "the repetition of the horizontal lines of land and sky," is very much in evidence in the Mussman landscape. The elm, ash, wild crabapple, plum, dogwood, poplar, and maple trees planted by the Mussmans are a reminder of

the civilizing force at work, yet do not interrupt the strongly horizontal lines of the garden. Long trellises at the far end of the garden, added each June for Marcia's pickling cucumbers, offer another echo of horizontal lines. The same trees that frame the vegetable garden were planted in other areas around the house to continue civilizing the vast open plain. In the woods, native flowers such as goldenrod (*Solidago*), shooting stars (*Dodecatheon*), violets (*Viola conspersa*), Joe Pye weed (*Eupatorium maculatum*), wild blue phlox (*Phlox divaricata*), and buttercups (*Ranunculus acris*) grow abundantly. Despite her efforts to transplant them into the garden itself, "they didn't like it, so I just go to the woods to enjoy them," says Marcia.

This garden does not have wooden borders around its raised beds. Here, where the temperature dips below zero and the soil freezes and thaws so consistently, Marcia finds that wooden frames around the beds tend to buckle. This convinced her that rather than trying to maintain a rigid definition of the beds with wooden boards, it was easier to plant directly into the earth and let the basil and other herbs that outline the beds spill over informally onto the grassy paths.

Despite the visual achievements of her vegetable garden, Marcia never forgets that the garden's primary purpose is to put vegetables on the family table. Vegetables may look beautiful together, but "they are planted," as she explains, "when the conditions are right for the individual vegetables. If beets and carrots need to go in at the same time, that is more important to me than trying to design beautifully contrasting textures." The block of 'Silver Queen' corn is bordered with bush beans, a collection of lima, wax, burgundy, and string beans. On the opposite side of the grassy path, balancing the block of corn, is an equally important block, intensively planted with several varieties of determinate tomatoes, supported by cages and also bordered with bush beans.

The asparagus harvest is a cause for celebration. Begun some 20 years ago, the crop is now so prolific that the Mussmans build a spring "Asparagus Party" around it: "We serve lots of asparagus with a choice of three different toppings: melted butter, hollandaise sauce, and poached eggs."

Even after 20 years of vegetable-gardening experience Marcia admits, "I marvel at how Nature has her own way of imposing herself onto my scheme. It makes it fun and challenging to know that I am never really in control of my own garden."

ASPARAGUS

(Asparagus officinalis)

Asparagus is one of the few perennial vegetables in the garden. If grown properly it will yield for years to come. (Marcia Mussman started her patch 20 years ago.)

WHEN
Start as soon as the ground can be worked in spring after all danger of frost is past.

WHERE
Plant crowns in full sun in a slightly acidic soil (pH 6.5–6.9) where they will not be disturbed. Soil must have good drainage.

HOW
Add rock phosphate or calcium phosphate at planting—it is the most needed nutrient. Keep crowns refrigerated until planting time, then soak them for at least an hour (not more than 12) before planting. Dig trenches 1 foot deep and 1½ feet wide, mounding compost, aged manure, and a balanced fertilizer in the bottom of each trench 1½ feet between crowns. Spread crowns out evenly 4–6 inches below ground level. Cover with 3 inches of soil and compost. Water.

CARE
As plants grows (spears may take as long as 3–8 weeks to appear), fill each trench gradually with soil and compost until level, never covering foliage. Mulch, weed, fertilize, and water plants. Do not harvest at all the first year, and harvest lightly the second and third years.

A Touch
of Jekyll
and Pride

INTERIOR AND GARDEN DESIGNERS BRUCE Burstert and the late Robert Raymond Smith of Kansas City, Missouri, while paying tribute to English gardening—as perceived in the work and writings of Gertrude Jekyll (whom they particularly admired), Penelope Hobhouse, and Rosemary Verey, as well as at Sissinghurst and many other English gardens—wanted to sound an American note.

On the one hand, Bruce had been greatly moved by the simple formality of the design of Monticello; on the other, he wanted to stress a certain looseness, a spontaneity, and, in particular, a softening of the design line through the abundance and richness of the plant material—a trait that had indeed become apparent in early American gardens and that, incidentally, had already revealed itself in Gertrude Jekyll's own English gardens. Accordingly, Bruce and Robert utilized a number of American plants, such as the purple coneflower (*Echinacea purpurea*), Turk's-cap lily (*Lilium superbum*), butterfly weed (*Asclepias tuberosa*), and the common purple morning glory, to name only a few. They also used materials with American associations for their accessories: a native cottonseed mulch made from by-products of the cottonseed industry, a handsome purple-brown pea gravel from the Missouri River for the paths, and old Kansas City paving stones for some of the borders.

During the ten years before Bruce and Robert started their own garden, they spent much of their time studying a multitude of books on gardening and garden design, both English and American. In addition to the above-mentioned English sources, they paid much attention to the works of 19th-century American garden designers Neltje Blanchan and Louise B. Wilder.

In 1991 the two men were able to acquire their house and its lot as well as three adjacent plots—amounting in all to under half an acre, an ideal size for a city garden. The Colonial Revival style of the house "dictated what the garden needed to be," Bruce explains, memories of Monticello inspiring them at least partially. Bruce and Robert did most of the work themselves and each took up specific responsibilities. Since he particularly enjoys cooking, the vegetable garden was Bruce's domain; the perennial section, Robert's.

Above: The pink and lavender tones permeating this garden heighten the beauty of the gray foliage in both the vegetables and the nonedible ornamentals. A section of the wattle fence surrounding the garden is visible in the background.

Right: Bruce Burstert, one of Kansas City's most respected interior and garden designers, loves the drama of the Brassica family, particularly in his Brussels sprouts that are far from low growing.

Above: *Before apples ripen in the fall, the English-inspired apple tunnel is covered with gourds and their decorative vines.*

The garden's layout is simple and totally symmetrical and is therefore quite formal. A circular bed marks the center. Four elongated trapezoidal beds form a square around it, and four long rectangular ones yet another square alongside the perimeter. The garden is enclosed on three sides by a wattle fence and its two arched entrances. The fourth side is delineated by an apple tunnel.

An early construction, the apple tunnel gives the garden its most important definition. It arches over a brick path starting just outside the kitchen door and separates vegetable and herb gardens. The path leads the visitor down a walkway—dappled in springtime—to the Jekyll-inspired perennial and woodland gardens. Several varieties of apple grow on the semicircular wooden arches, and in summer and fall the tunnel is festooned with decorative gourds and their vines. The idea is presented in Gertrude Jekyll's *Garden Ornament* of 1918, but it was specifically inspired by a similar "fruit pergola" at New Place, Oxfordshire, reproduced in Penelope Hobhouse's *Garden Style* of 1988. In winter when the zone 5 temperature drops below zero, the beautiful structure frequently offers a dramatic outline against the snow.

Around the same time as the tunnel, another important element of the garden's bones was being put into place: the wattle fence. Like their colonial predecessors, Bruce and Robert took advantage of branches from the trees that were felled in the initial clearing of the property. Colonial Americans found wattle convenient for protecting their vegetable gardens from the barnyard animals. It became a common feature in the American landscape and remained so until the end of the 19th century—when timber was milled on a grand scale in the 1880s and sawmills dotted the countryside, the picket fence all but replaced the wattle.

Above: *Nothing could be simpler than this arrangement of native American coneflowers and a head of ruffled kale brought indoors to capture the sunlight of a midsummer afternoon. Overleaf: Granite paving stones that once lined the Kansas City streets in the 1860s now edge and help raise the central bed as well as the rectilinear side beds. The Ionic-style capital, found in Iowa, punctuates the center of the garden while adding a note of classic formality—and an American one at that.*

Bruce found inspiration for his fence in William Lawson's drawing from *A New Orchard and Garden*, published in 1618. Whereas traditional English and American wattle fences are made of willow branches that are held together mostly with mud mortar, and some of which need to be replaced every year, Bruce's is made of longer-lasting walnut, mulberry, and linden branches that are simply interwoven.

Hidden away behind the 6-foot-high wattle fence, near the compost pile and toolshed, is an area Bruce has devoted to tomatoes and other "dirty vegetables" that do not fit into his formal garden plan—or into the color scheme.

Eight gooseberry topiaries symmetrically accent the circular layout of the garden's center section and offer an understated reminder that the basic design is highly formal. It was not by accident that Bruce chose the gooseberry for his topiaries. It is quite hardy and well suited to zone 5's climate. Besides, it requires no care other than the regular annual mulching given all the vegetables at the end of the growing season.

Leeks, in combination with the equally long lasting Brussels sprouts, contribute to maintaining the garden's dominant color late in the growing season. 'St. Victor', a strain of the old French heirloom leek 'Bleu de Solaise' (available from Shepherd's Garden Seeds; see Source List), in particular, adds its own subdued blue note to that of the sprouts, in keeping with the blue-gray tone of the full-summer garden, when it is still brimming with the bluish cabbages and kale as well as gray and gray-green artichoke and cardoon fronds, woolly thyme, verbascum, dianthus foliage, and sage.

The Brussels sprouts themselves offer one of the most felicitous notes of the garden's design. On the one hand, their own proportions are pleasing even when their stalks are at their maximum height of 3 feet. Perhaps more important, however, they provide a blue-green border between the taller, darker wattle fence and the central circular bed, in which the strawberry rim, no less than the pale pink dianthus and, later in the season, zinnias, provides a luminous contrast with the predominantly green leeks and herbs.

There is more than a touch of magic to the garden. When one enters it through one of the high, rather somber arches in the wattle fence, one is impressed by the freshness, elegant forms, and subtle color harmonies of the plants as well as by the apparent simplicity of the design. One has the impression of passing through the gateway of an imaginary earlier period, a time when tranquillity and serenity prevailed. Once again one is reminded of Gertrude Jekyll: "The first purpose of a garden," she wrote, "is to be a place of quiet beauty such as will give delight to the eye and repose and refreshment to the mind."

Left: *The apple tunnel divides the vegetables on the left from the herbs on the right.*

BRUSSELS SPROUTS

(Brassica oleracea, Gemmifera group)

Well worth growing for their flavor and their high vitamin C content, as well as for their unique decorative addition to the garden, home-grown Brussels sprouts are far superior to those sold commercially. They take a long time to mature (as much as 100–200 days), although they taste sweeter with a touch of frost, which also reduces aphid damage.

WHEN
Start seeds indoors in spring in cold-winter regions or in early to midsummer in mild-winter areas. (Bruce Burstert in Kansas City starts his in a cold frame in mid-March.)

WHERE
Grow in full sun in a slightly acidic soil (pH above 6.0) composted and amended with aged manure.

HOW
Sow seed ½ inch deep. Move young sprouts from the cold frame into the garden in late May when they are about 3 inches tall. Transplant (or if seeded directly in spring thin to) 18 inches apart, and give them 2 feet between rows or a good square foot per plant. Rotate crops to control disease, as with other cabbages.

CARE
Treat plants similarly to broccoli and kale (see pages 54 and 105). Add a well-balanced fertilizer (one with plenty of nitrogen) at least once a month during the long growing season. Keep soil well weeded and consistently moist (1 inch of water every week from rain or by watering).

The Cultivated
and
the Wild

KAREN STROHBEEN AND BILL LUCHSINGER'S 8-acre garden on their 80-acre farm in south-central Iowa is not only beautiful but remarkably *American*. While Karen and Bill have captured the "Prairie Style" in their wild yet controlled garden, its design is based on their own extraordinary knowledge of horticulture, a profound respect for preservation, a love of the midwestern landscape and its native plants, and their combined artistic sense of plant harmony. At their farm, a stylized meadow of grasses and wildflowers—including butterfly weed (*Asclepias tuberosa*), rattlesnake master (*Eryngium yuccifolium*), 'Little' and 'Big' bluestems (*Schizachyrium*), pussy-toes (*Anennaria neglecta*), and a rare native hibiscus (*Militaris*)—reaches out to join the woods of native oaks and cottonwood trees on the horizon, while their man-made, bass-filled pond separates the wildness of the prairie landscape from the lush, cultivated garden closer to the house. Karen remarks, "It is that tension between the cultivated and the wild that makes our garden special."

Originally Bill found a Japanese giant silver banner grass (*Miscanthus sacchariflorus*) in the meadow on the far side of the pond, and to it he added native grasses to both the meadow and their cultivated garden closer to the house, where most of the Strohbeen-Luchsinger energy is spent. They rejected as inappropriate the idea of a traditional garden laid out on a central axis and instead designed the beds to repeat the graceful contours of the rolling hillside. Flowers (both perennial and annual), vegetables, and ornamental grasses are dramatically mixed together in each of the curving beds that reach toward the house and sweep between grassy paths stretching from the banks of the pond right up to those near the house. Indeed, the breathtaking beauty of the long view only enhances the near at hand: a mixture of beautifully grown vegetables and perennials, all carefully combined in a loose, unstructured, free-flowing way.

These two native Iowans are true gardeners and till the soil today much as their grandparents did. Karen's maternal grandfather grew vegetables and homeopathic herbs, which he used at the sanitarium he presided over two generations ago; her Dutch-German paternal grandparents were dedicated farmers who became role models for her

Above: *In their Iowa garden, Bill Luchsinger and Karen Strohbeen, both accomplished artists and gardeners, have created a garden that is at the same time unique and truly American. It brims with native grasses, flowers—both wild and cultivated—and their favorite vegetables are tucked in with a flair that is as free as their unbounded imaginations.* Right: *The most manicured part of the garden clearly shows the importance of meticulous grooming in growing vegetables that look as stunning as they are delicious. The 24 boxes of flowers and vegetables are as beautiful in their own way as the wildest part beyond the lake.*

Left: *Karen and Bill dig their sweet potatoes carefully in order to save the attractive purple foliage of* Ipomoea batatas *'Blacky' that will continue to enhance the beauty of the area.*

Right: *'Ruby Red' chard teams with red rugosa 'Linda Campbell' roses and echoes the lavender hues of the neighboring* Aster frikartii *'Monch'.* Left: *Fennel bulb and flowers match and contrast with* Lysimachia nummularia *'Aurea' (moneywort).*

SWISS CHARD

(Beta vulgaris, Cicla group*)*

Although beets and chard are of the same species, they are grown for different edible parts: beets for roots, and chard for leafy foliage that is rich in vitamin A. Chard is one of the easier vegetables to grow. Plants mature in 55–60 days.

WHEN
Plant anytime from early spring to early summer after all danger of frost is past. In mild-winter areas, chard will winter over but will bolt the following spring.

WHERE
In all zones, sow seeds in full sun, in well-composted, well-spaded soil, ½–¾ inch deep.

HOW
Direct-seed, then thin seedlings to 12 inches apart.

CARE
Water consistently and keep well weeded. Harvest outer leaves 2 months after sowing.

as a child. In addition, Karen attributes her respect for doing things in an orderly fashion to her engineer-trained father. As for the other member of the team, Bill says it was his Irish grandmother who instilled in him a love of gardening and a profound respect for the land.

Both gardeners bring their fine-arts background into the creation of new and pleasing color combinations of flowers with vegetables and in taking advantage of the powers and subtleties of these combinations. For example, the red of the barn was the inspiration for combining 'Ruby Red' chard with late-summer zinnias and dark, garnet red—almost black—hollyhocks. Touches of purple heliotrope enliven the bed with another hue, echoing the soft purple underside of sweet potato leaves and the deeper shade of the magenta clematis that makes a wonderful ground cover when allowed to ramble.

Except for radishes and carrots, which are later planted directly in the ground, all of the vegetables are started in the greenhouse in February, then moved outdoors to begin their climb up the tepee supports or nestled in among the perennials about 45 days later, when the soil reaches 70 degrees. The tepees are fashioned from thin, dark green poles that fit neatly into the four corners of the 4-foot by 4-foot box beds and are moved around from year to year according to the rotation of crops and to the new experiments in seemingly limitless color combinations Karen and Bill have dreamed up: leeks with lettuce, feathery fennel next to chartreuse lady's-mantle (*Alchemilla mollis*), and deep purple eggplant next to a golden barberry shrub (*Berberis* 'Aurea'). By June the cucumbers are ready to pick from vines that ramble up next to clematis vines. By September sweet potatoes will be dug, lightly brushed with oil, baked into crisp chips, and served to guests.

Above: *A view of the greenhouse, where most of the plants are started at Karen and Bill's farm. A section of their imaginative vegetable boxes in July demonstrates that textural contrasts are as important as those of color in creating a beautiful vegetable garden. Different stages of the plants' cycle involve the viewer in the pleasure of anticipating what is still to come.*

Vegetables harvested from May until after the first frost include tomatoes, peppers, carrots, leeks, onions, and dozens of lettuce varieties. Cleome, hollyhocks, and a climbing clematis (*Clematis* × *jackmanii*) turn up in the neighboring boxes to complement the colors and textures of the vegetables. Karen has juxtaposed a variety of foliage in the sweet potatoes, asparagus, cardoon,

and corn throughout the garden to enhance the long view and to provide imaginative detailed interest at close range as well.

"Each garden has to relate to the larger landscape," she says, "and though color is the most important organizing element, we learn each year that some plants do particularly well together."

Vegetables on the Rocks

OF ALL THE BEAUTIFUL VEGETABLE GARDENS in America, none has a more compatible connection with its surroundings than that of Ann and Sigurd Anderson at their Lake Vermilion island home (Øyheim in Norwegian) in northern Minnesota. One day in 1980, shortly after their cedar cabin was finished (in an appropriate, clean-lined Scandinavian style), the Andersons began to clear the extensive scrub brush from the sunniest area on their 4-acre island, out of the shade of the native white pines and silver birch. They wanted a small vegetable garden where they would grow "just the basics," but with a determination to grow the most beautiful vegetables with the least possible disturbance to the natural habitat. They agree that there were no great plans for the garden in the beginning; the primary goal was to reduce the number of hour-long trips by boat and by car for "a few abused and wizened vegetables at the nearest supermarket."

As Sig and Ann, with the help of their neighbor, Nora Carron Esselstrom, cleared away piles of brush, they began to uncover some natural outcroppings of beautiful gray-green ledge rock, one of the components in the indigenous rock formations, known as the "Knife Lakes Structure." They also found 12 shallow crypts of the same metamorphic rock that would later serve as handsome planting pockets. That first summer they sifted out the rocks spalled from the indigenous ledge rock, added a few nutrients to the humus left from 10,000 years of wind drift, and began their first island garden. Initially, the garden consisted of a few scallions and lettuces in the first of the "pockets." Today there is hardly a vegetable that this experienced gardening couple doesn't grow.

Because of its location and orientation, a portion of the garden is in partial shade all day, but the nearby native birch, balsam, and cedar trees provide such a dramatic background for the vegetable garden that they have been largely left untouched. Soft grassy slopes frame the other three sides of the garden. Fortunately, the garden is in a sun trap, where even such warm-season vegetables as tomatoes, Oriental eggplant, and peppers grow successfully. The Andersons found that the reflected heat of the rocks is a particular help in growing the heat-loving 'Bell Boy' peppers. "The vegetables don't spring forward as they do in Iowa and other

Above: *The peppermint-striped 'Italian Chioggia' beets from Shepherd's Seeds grow particularly well in the summer garden at Øyheim (which means "island home" in Norwegian).* Right: *The beautiful gray-green ledge rock typical of the "Knife Lakes Structure" in northern Minnesota provides a dramatic structural background for Ann and Sig Anderson's vegetables. Curly kale, collards, and leeks nestle in the pockets of enriched soil prepared by the Andersons.*

CABBAGES

Cabbage (*Brassica oleracea*, Capitata group) and Chinese Cabbage *(B. Rapa*, Pekinensis group)

According to the horticulturists at Mount Vernon and Monticello, both George Washington and Thomas Jefferson grew cone-shaped cabbage in their gardens. Today other varieties include early-, mid-, and late-season types such as green- and red-ball cabbage and 'Savoy', with loose, wavy, crinkled leaves.

WHEN

Start indoors 8 weeks before the last hard frost in short-season zones. In milder zones, sow seeds directly in early spring. For a fall crop, start seeds in July or August. Cabbage usually takes 60–90 days to mature.

WHERE

Grow in full sun, in well-drained, richly composted soil. Add commercially aged turkey manure to the entire garden for best results.

HOW

Start seeds outdoors in a cold frame with a strong light source, in a flat of planting mix. Cover seeds ¼ inch deep. Transplant seedlings into a deeper pot and harden plants off. Around Memorial Day, transplant pots to the garden at least 2 feet apart. To stagger harvest times, sow some seeds directly in garden.

CARE

Water generously and provide a good supply of nitrogen. To control insect and soilborne diseases, rotate cabbage at least every four years to a different, non-Brassica bed. Feed at 2-week intervals with a well-balanced fertilizer and keep weeded and well watered.

warmer parts of the country," Ann explains. "Here, in zone 3, they just grow slowly and steadily, producing a continuous bounty. We are lucky because the water around the island is warmer than the air, and the warming effect protects us from early and late frosts. Our growing season is extended on both ends to a surprising degree." Although the season is short, Ann and Sig do plant successively some of the favorites that grow especially well on the island: lettuces and beans that last all summer, as well as beets, carrots, and turnips, which are seeded directly into the pockets, filling in the bare spots as the other vegetables are harvested.

While the vegetables are planted in combinations according to how much they will shade their neighbors, the visual compatibility of textures, shapes, and colors is an even more important consideration. But the primary appeal of this 80-foot free-form garden comes mainly from the natural way in which the garden contours follow the natural topography of the land. It slopes gently down on three levels and is irregularly patterned by horizontal slashes of outcroppings, by hollowed-out crypts, and by a collage of stone borders and steppingstones connecting the pockets of different vegetables. The randomness in the overall design is artfully in keeping with the ruggedness of a terrain that reveals the fascinating scars of millennia of geologic change. Where the ledge rock is exposed in this garden, it offers a wonderfully strong contrast to the delicate new lettuces, carrots, herbs, and tender vegetables in the pockets of the garden. Only the massive blue cabbages stand defiantly strong against the impressive rock formations. By echoing the same gray-green color tones of the rocks, the softly

Right: The boldness of the 'Butter Stick' squash and cabbage leaves is heightened by the feathery lightness of dill and Italian parsley tucked into the rock basins of Ann and Sig Anderson's terraced garden.

Above: 'Yellow Finn', 'Peruvian Blue', and 'Royo' potatoes from Seeds Blum "sets" were scrubbed while still new and cooked the same day. Potato blossoms and purple basil will continue to grow throughout the summer, while scattered Johnny-jump-ups add to the aesthetic delight of the entire Anderson garden. Left: Ann and Sigurd Anderson sit on one of the indigenous rocky outcroppings that form the dramatic structure of their island vegetable garden on Lake Vermilion, Minnesota.

curled kales and cabbages emphasize their own fragility and are a dramatic reminder of the transitoriness of the garden and of all living things. Whenever they could, the Andersons moved the rocks with log chains and winches or rolled them into position. When the rocks were impossibly heavy, they were simply left where nature placed them or split in two. The garden was then imaginatively formed around the rocks. "Always our goal is to make the garden a pretty picture, and sometimes it is prettier than at other times. We rotate every year for the same reason other gardeners do—to help the vegetables to a change of soils, which they need," Ann explains.

Anywhere from mid-May to Memorial Day, as soon as the ice is gone, the Andersons drive up from Iowa with a carload of provisions, including seeds, vegetable and flower seedlings started in their Des Moines cold frame, and a good load of aged turkey manure as well. This fabulous natural addition is mixed in late spring with the layers of dried leaves, humus, bonemeal, and compost, all of which filled the vegetable pockets at the end of the previous summer and were left to mellow under 4 feet of ice during the winter months. Ann Anderson offers a 20th-century testimony for the durability of rhubarb, one of the oldest medicinal roots, dating back to 2700 B.C. China: "You can drive a car over the ice and yet the rhubarb in our garden winters over!"

While most of the vegetable seeds come from Shepherd's Garden Seeds or The Cook's Garden, Sig and Ann buy their cabbage seeds from a variety of sources: an excellent Early Flathead Dutch variety started in their cold frame comes from The D. Landreth Seed Company (see Source List); Iowa-based Earl May Garden Center has their favorite 'Danish Ball' green cabbage, the Savoy comes from Northrup King; and the beautiful red Japanese variety 'Scarlet O'Hara Red' is from Shepherd's. They stagger their early-, mid-, and late-season varieties not only because cabbages grow spectacularly well at Øyheim, but, like the Minnesota scenery, it is a reminder of Sigurd Anderson's Norwegian roots. Ann, an excellent cook, prepares this Scandinavian staple in a variety of ways, including those recipes handed down from Sig's family.

Perhaps more than any other vegetable, potatoes are a house specialty. "Potatoes are so fundamental and seem to have been sadly relegated to the category of the mundane. Yet there are as many possibilities for the potato as there are for chicken," Ann believes. "This is a vegetable that should be grown at home in order to get the full nutritional value and its superb flavor." She bakes, steams, and sautés them. One of her favorite methods is to scrub them clean the same day they are dug, then brush them with just a little olive oil, and slice and bake them for about half an hour in a gratin dish. Sometimes she sprinkles on a little chopped onion. "Then before serving we add a bit of chopped parsley or other herbs. It's amazing how little it takes when they are fresh." The Anderson selection of 'Yellow Finn', 'Giant Peanut Fingerlings', and the virus-free mini-tuber 'All-Blue' are all from Shepherd's.

A few edible flowers such as nasturtiums and Johnny-jump-ups come forth as volunteers here and there, adding their random charm to the blossoming vines of the various squash, potatoes, and scarlet runner beans. Only those are permitted to clamber over and among the rocks in this exclusively edible garden. Anything more would be out of keeping with the extraordinary control that Ann and Sig Anderson have exercised in preserving their garden in its unique and natural beauty.

the

FAR WEST

"She from old fountains doth new judgment draw,/ Till, word by word, the ancient order swerves/
To the true course more nigh; in every age/ A little she creates, but more preserves."

GEORGE E. WOODBERRY, "MY COUNTRY," 1903

The Ultimate Mix

blessed with a climate more nearly like that of Naples than of Boston, Atlanta, or Minneapolis, Californians have always gardened with a sense of history that blends North American, Mediterranean, and Latin traditions. In northern California and the Pacific Northwest, where fog and rain and generally moderate temperatures produce a climate that has much in common with the British Isles and the immigrant population comes as often from the Far East as from Europe, gardeners are masters of innovation. Along the Pacific Coast, the unexpected is to be expected.

Several of the gardeners featured here have adapted French gardening traditions to their own specifications—raising their planting beds, dividing their gardens into formal parterres. Others have followed a mix-and-match method, planting what they like and what grows well in their own particular subclimate.

Whatever they are spared in struggling with the weather extremes of New England and the South, Californians suffer in periodic drought and searing Santa Ana winds. Like gardeners everywhere, they work with the weather and treasure the bounty of their beautiful vegetable gardens.

Parterres—
American
Style

WITH THE SANTA YNEZ MOUNTAINS framing the view beyond the garden, apple orchard, and horse pastures of Malcolm and Mary McDuffie's 4-acre farm in Santa Barbara, the setting could be nowhere else but southern California. Yet there is also the hint of a European sophistication that echoes native Californian Mary de Surville McDuffie's French background. The classic order, taste, and logic associated with the gardens of 17th-century France, the grand ones as well as the small *jardins de curé*, or curates' gardens, inform this country garden as much as the California climate.

For the design, the McDuffies chose Isabelle Greene, a California landscape architect with an in-depth knowledge and love of native plant material but who is also known for her sensitivity in matching the garden to the client. "I remember Mary's description of the first time she saw this property—with a horse and an old-fashioned hayrack coming down the lane," Isabelle recalls. "Anything more formal than a quiet country garden would have been inappropriate, even though it is in a very sophisticated suburban area."

The magnificent view of the mountains from all parts of the garden was a main consideration for the design, and yet a central axis that would connect the house and pool on a lower level straight up to the garden and dramatically focus on the limitless vista of the mountains in the distance would have "lifted this garden up to be *the grand garden* and that it is *not*," Isabelle explains. "So we gave it its own termination, using a small 17th-century sundial that Mary and Malcolm brought back from England, on its own patch of decomposed granite that melts away into the shapeless side beds. And then there is the apple fence to stop the eye." To further offset the idea of a central axis being the dominant line of the garden, the vegetable garden is off to one side, with its own separate axial line symmetrically dividing the boxes, which, carefully placed on diagonals from the garden's main axis, take maximum advantage of the space.

The gently weathered redwood boxes, designed by Malcolm McDuffie and called her *parterres de broderie* by Mary, are handsome enough in themselves—all finely finished with a 4-inch hand-hewn ledge that is

Above: *The corners and sides of the handsome wooden planting boxes designed by Malcolm McDuffie are mitered to perfection and call to mind the order, logic, and precision characteristic of rational thinking at the height of the golden age in France.*

Right: *Mary de Surville McDuffie with a tall and skinny Monterey pear tree on her 4-acre farm in Santa Barbara. The pear and a crisscross of espaliered apple trees at the rear of the garden suggest Mary's French Normandy background.*

Above: *In this French California garden, the McDuffies have used decomposed granite—a neutral beige material that sets off the flowers and vegetables in the same way gravel was used by André LeNôtre in classical French gardens. It blends nicely with the large sand-colored indigenous boulders and stone edging in the garden, and is more practical for frequent wheelbarrow crossings and easier to maintain than the French equivalent. The Belgian "Doublet" apple fence in the background separates the main vegetable garden from its annex.*

wide enough to sit on while harvesting or working in the beds.

Even when empty and waiting for the next refurbishment of the McDuffie special soil, which is done with each planting, the boxes, gently rising according to the slight grading of the land, are so harmoniously related through the compatibility of their shapes (all are the same width and height but vary slightly in length and geometric form) they stand almost as sculptures. When not full of various vegetables—including chevron-patterned lettuces, radicchio and contrasting dark leafed

spinach, dwarf patio tomatoes (in perfect scale for the 3-foot-wide beds), carrots, Japanese eggplant, and an abundance of parsley, chives, chervil, basil, and other herbs—the beds are always kept raked and well manicured by the able custodians of the garden, Claire Gottsdanker and Marcia Bellinger, and formerly by the late Chole Morgan, a dedicated plantsman who contributed so much.

Mary de Surville McDuffie remembers the apple fence at the de Surville family domain near Pont l'Eveque in Normandy and wanted one for her Santa Barbara garden.

With the help of Ray Sodomka, a local nurseryman, Isabelle Greene designed a fence based on an old Belgian one. "Doublet," as Isabelle named it, refers not to an article of clothing but to "one of a pair" because *two* apple whips are planted in the same hole and so tilted, tied (with rebar reinforcements), and pruned so as to create a diamond weave or crisscross of espaliered apple trees. Eventually, aided by incisions, they become grafted together where they cross, forming a latticelike screen of apple blossoms in the spring and apples in the fall. Two-year-old semidwarf 'Pettingill' apple whips—their tips untrimmed for maximum early growth—were used.

In the spring and summer the apple fence defines the back of the 44-by-20-foot vegetable garden and separates it from "the annex," where the more rambunctious vegetables such as squash, tomatoes, cucumbers, melons, and lots of *haricots verts* (green beans) are allowed to climb and sprawl and luxuriate in the California sun.

Even in the annex garden there is a nod to formality in the wrought-iron arbor covered by the 'New Dawn' rose, flanked by roses on one side and vegetables on the other. Here in full sun a double tepee trellis connected by rows of string offers the French string beans plenty of air circulation and an easy climb. They are an unassuming background for the thickly planted scallions, peppers, tomatoes, and melons in front (both the Israeli variety 'Ogen' and Malcolm McDuffie's favorite, Burpee's 'Ambrosia', a thick-fleshed cantaloupe that "is the best cantaloupe I ever tasted").

While one would never confuse the 4-acre citrus-lined McDuffie farm in the heart of increasingly urban Montecito with a French garden or even a Normandy farm, the indigenous plants and boulders and the special setting combined with touches of classical French design make for a happy country garden.

CARROTS

(Daucus carota var. *sativus)*

Plant different varieties of seeds for a long season beginning in June and continuing through September. For an ongoing harvest, plant every 2 weeks. Carrots, like beets and other root crops, usually take up to 90 days to mature.

WHEN
In California, start carrots in mid-March and continue throughout the summer and fall. Elsewhere, plant in early spring 1–2 weeks before the first frost-free date. Seeds can take up to 3 weeks to germinate.

WHERE
Plant in full sun in fertile soil that is well drained. The soil must be well dug before planting, as roots become distorted when they run into rocks or clumps in the soil.

HOW
Sow seeds directly ¼–½ inch deep and ½ inch apart in rows 6 inches apart, or plant in blocks for a feathery contrast next to blocks of lettuce (as the McDuffies do). Cover with a thin layer of compost.

CARE
For carrots to develop evenly, keep the soil moist and weed free. Do not use fresh manure. Harvest carrots before they protrude aboveground and grow green and bitter. At the McDuffie garden Claire corrects alkaline soil with soil sulfur mixed with fresh soil and blood meal before planting. Mix new compost into the soil with every successive planting.

A Vintner's Vegetables

SOME 30 YEARS AGO, DESIGNER AND AUTHOR and co-owner with her husband of the family winery, Chappellet, Molly Chappellet was very much impressed by the vegetable garden designed by the late Leland Noel for her friend Maggie Wetzel (see pages 156–159). "His genius was to put the garden in exactly the right place," says Molly. The Chappellets moved their vegetable garden to the sunniest side of their property on the slope of the hill, laying it out along three semicircular terraces that curve gracefully around a large oak tree, thus making the oak the dramatic focal point of the garden. The terraces are buttressed by walls of rough-hewn rocks that blend with the landscape. Over the years the garden was extended beneath the terraces, which look out onto the vineyard below. From a patio in the shade of the oak, the Chappellets' family and guests enjoy the seasonal color changes of the Chardonnay and Cabernet vineyards below, a spectacular view of Lake Hennessey in the distance, and the ever-changing shapes and hues of the sky.

In early spring, the vines bud out and the hillside all around becomes carpeted in a sparkling chartreuse green. In the late summer and fall, the grape leaves turn gold, yellow, orange, burgundy, and deep purple. These, together with the colors of the sunset, offered a palette for the garden that allowed Molly to marry the Napa Valley landscape with her man-made garden.

The Chappellets knew that the new site chosen by Noel had been a veritable rock quarry and were skeptical at first. Their daughter Lygia contributed one of the first components of the design by painstakingly gathering and stacking the rocks to build the wall of what was to become the highest terrace of the garden. When her father, Donn, came to appreciate what she was creating, heavy equipment was brought in to clear away some of the rocks, to complete her wall and build the other two.

But there remained the rocks and boulders, which were a source of frustration every time Molly wanted to plant a tree or till the soil for a bed of vegetables. Eventually, she came to terms with them and recognized that not only could the larger boulders *not* be moved, but, happily, they would enhance the whole design and add an austere dignity that few man-made ornaments could ever equal.

One of the most ingenious features of the Chappellet garden is utilitarian. It is a 4-foot-wide compost trench

Above. *The best pumpkin for making soup, according to Molly Chappellet, is a French one, 'Mme. Curie', shown here dramatically lit in the intense California sunshine— one of the prerequisites for lush, tasty pumpkins and* squash. Right. *Summer squash such as this giant white 'Pattypan', as well as pumpkins and winter squash, respond well to the manure and compost added to the soil earlier in the year.*

Left: *The shape and texture of a single artichoke when it is allowed to blossom or even to dry is uniquely beautiful.*

Right: *Shades of the Napa Valley in the fall are captured in the spectacular display of pumpkins and winter squash on the terrace overlooking the vegetable garden and beyond to the Napa foothills.*

that curves between two rows of the vineyard adjacent to the vegetable garden, is invisible from the patio, and is easily accessible from both garden and vineyard. In it are collected cuttings, leaves, and vegetable waste. Out of it comes a superb soil to be generously scattered over the entire garden. At times tendrils from nearby pumpkin vines create their own magic, embellishing another compost "holding" trench with a decorative embroidery, while tall artichoke stalks provide a golden screen through which to peer at the distant blue-to-violet hills.

In the early 1970s, feeding Donn and Molly's six children in addition to the increasing number of guests at the winery who enjoyed the warm Chappellet hospitality meant that a vegetable garden was practically a necessity —particularly since the garden was far closer to the kitchen than the nearest market some 25 minutes away. Each year the semicircular terraces filled up with tomatoes, beans, parsnips, lettuce, carrots, spinach, cabbages, and corn, among many other vegetables. Over the years the garden grew farther beyond the terraces; herbs tumbled over the walls; more flowers were added to enhance the beauty of the vegetables; the pumpkin vines rambled farther afield; the volunteer artichokes sent forth their silvery fronds here and there; the raspberry trellises and the flower fields demanded their own space; and more corn was planted because it looked so beautiful in harmony with the purple amaranth and the sunset. In time, the garden became what it is today: 2 acres of beautifully grown flowers, vegetables, trees, and shrubs that blend with each other and spill into the hillside around them.

While the garden as a whole looks as if nature itself had spontaneously planted it, every detail reflects careful planning and an unerring sense of order. The curving paths, covered with porous black crushed grape seeds, are elegantly related to the rock walls; boulders and rocks contribute unifying rhythms. The flowers and vegetables harmonize within each pocket of related hues and contrast ingeniously with neighboring pockets.

As the garden expanded, Molly's designer's eye focused on the limitless decorative possibilities of certain vegetables, particularly in the Cucurbita family. She started with a few named varieties, but over the years, by saving the seeds, her collection has grown in the measure of her unbounded enthusiasm for the whole squash/ pumpkin/gourd family. Currently, the nubby celadon green 'Blue Hubbard' variety is one of her favorites; it can become, through natural hybridization with its neighboring white pumpkins in the field, an equally elegant smooth-textured celadon green. Molly also grows the dark turquoise 'Queensland Blue', a variety that best embodies the taxonomist's dilemma when trying to categorize certain cucurbits: it is called a pumpkin in Australia, its country of origin, but became classified in America as a winter squash.

Only recently have white pumpkins—grown and appreciated by Molly for many years—become increasingly popular, and more easily available through seed catalogs. Her immaculate specimens, of all sizes and shapes, are stunningly effective in her tabletop arrangements and provide decorative highlights in the garden. Their flavor is so delicate that she almost refrains from adding onions to her white pumpkin soup in order to let the elusive taste come through. The seeds of three varieties are available through catalogs: 'Lumina', 'Flat White Boer', and 'Cheesequake' (see page 183). A white squash

Following pages: *Varying shades of orange, rust, and yellow marigolds planted in a courageous juxtaposition with vivid purple verbena. As elsewhere in the garden, ornamental annuals and biennials are mixed in with beans, cabbage, and dark green kale. A yellow-blossomed ailanthus tree completes the vibrant-hued fall garden when it is at its best.*

WINTER SQUASH

Winter Squash and Pumpkins (*Cucurbita pepo*
and *C. maxima*)

Pumpkin and winter squash culture is similar to that of gourds; all
require a longer growing season (90–120 days to maturity), more
moisture, and more consistently sunny days than summer squash.

WHEN
Direct-seed in late May or early June (as Molly Chappellet
does in California).

WHERE
Both pumpkins and winter squash need maximum sunlight
and rich, moist earth.

HOW
Plant seeds directly in the soil (½–1 inch deep, 4–8 feet apart), or in
hills (6 seeds to a hill, each 4–8 feet apart), after all danger of frost
is past and the soil is warm (70–95°F).

CARE
No additional fertilizer is necessary once the soil has been prepared
with a good mulch of rich compost. It is best to direct-seed, but winter squash and pumpkins can be started indoors 4–5 weeks before
the last frost date. Avoid transplant shock by planting seeds in peat
pots, then setting seedlings, pots and all, in the garden. For large,
exhibition-size fruit, allow only one pumpkin on each plant to mature.

that should be mentioned as another decorative accent is
the 'White Swan' acorn squash (*Cucurbita pepo*). Pumpkin growers all over the country share the same fascina-
tion with this versatile Cucurbita family and its ability to
render an astonishing number of new varieties.

A few varieties that look beautiful in the garden are
also grown for their unique tastes. 'Pearl Blue'—which
has a tinge of peach coming though a smooth, pale blue-
green skin—and the large, smooth, peach-colored 'Pink
Banana' offer a delicious fleshy meat and, like most
pumpkins and winter squash, are rich in beta carotene.
The striped 'Cushaw' (nicknamed sweet potato squash)
and the smaller 'Delicata' varieties offer a variegated
accent in the Cucurbita collection.

The pumpkins take center stage in Molly Chappellet's
garden from September until the first frost. Afterward the
chartreuse 'Romanesca' broccoli provides a vivid contrast with the purple amaranth; red-leafed lettuces, radicchio, and the last of the carrots, turnips, and other root
vegetables add their various shades of green to the winter
landscape. Parsnips often sweetened by the frost continue to delight the Chappellets' guests until the first of
March when signs of spring appear. Shortly, it will be
time to begin anew but—for Molly Chappellet—always
in an imaginatively different way from the year before.

Right: *A Japanese persimmon tree 'Hachiya' in September. It is grown
for the culinary as well as the ornamental pleasure it provides.*

Vegetables on Center Stage

THE MOOD INGENIOUSLY CREATED IN Virginia Wyman's and Joe McDonnal's garden is at once festive and dramatic. Joe McDonnal, the garden's designer and part owner, achieved the ambiance through an incongruous but triumphant mixture of exotic and familiar plants, a few dramatic yet well-chosen garden structures and accessories, and a carefully worked out design involving three levels. Sometimes at twilight it looks more like a romantic stage set than "a country cottage garden in downtown Seattle," as Joe describes his garden, where vegetables grow almost incidentally in it.

Virginia, a full-time community volunteer and philanthropist, and Joe, a chef, caterer, restaurant owner, and party designer, are too busy to maintain a conventional vegetable garden: "Vegetable gardens are wonderful, but it is very disappointing to have one that is not really properly taken care of. We don't grow all the vegetables every year because they are so time-consuming and we have such wonderful vegetable purveyors at the Seattle public market. We couldn't possibly match what they grow. Nevertheless, I love having a garden in which vegetables add their own unique decoration."

Nothing from the front of the suburban house in this very integrated neighborhood would suggest that an almost surreal garden lies beyond the traditional ivy-covered fence. Starting in 1982 with a mud lot enclosed by a cyclone fence sloping away from the house, Virginia and Joe acquired another seven adjoining lots in 1985 and 1986, creating a lush, well-conceived garden property.

Although only 80 feet long and 45 feet wide, the main garden appears much larger because Joe cleverly avoided straight lines—except for the space-defining cyclorama of tall poplar trees at the bottom of the garden and the 60-foot-long ivy-covered retaining wall that separates the second terrace from the third. Instead of the usual strong axial line stretching the length of the garden, 12 arches curve over a graveled pathway that zigs and zags through parterres of colorful flowers and vegetables all crowded happily together in oddly shaped geometric sections.

The views of the entire garden from afar—whether from the terrace outside the dining room or from the pagoda-like structure above the pool that Joe and Virginia call their "picnic house," or the surprising vistas through the trees down onto the garden—are what most

Above: Oriental hybrid lilies must share the limelight with 22 varieties of summer squash, tomatoes, and brightly colored peppers that thrive along with the flowers in Joe McDonnal's and Virginia Wyman's Seattle garden. Right: The garden is so attractive to passersby that neighborhood children could not resist taking a splash in the pool on a hot summer afternoon —at first uninvited, but later not only invited three afternoons a week at regular hours but also provided with a lifeguard.

enchant visitors. Like Joe and Virginia, the garden is expansive and generous, a setting designed to amuse and entertain their friends. Twenty-six of the 40 varieties of lilac trees were bought on one extravagant shopping spree and now provide a dazzling cloudlike canopy of lavender, purple, white, pink, and mauve blossoms in the spring at the back of the highest of the three terraces.

There is something charmingly outlandish about a man who says with emphatic modesty, "I'm not a real gardener; I'm a faux-gardener. And I hate gardens that are perfectly edged, with not a single weed, where every blade of grass is pointed toward Mecca. They make me nervous. Everything that wants to is allowed to grow here—volunteers that have come to live with us, or even weeds." (Fortunately, the flowers and vegetables are so intensive that usually there is no room for these.)

"We wanted every color you could think of—like at a festival or carnival!" Although Joe McDonnal's garden reflects that same exuberantly colorful point of view, there is, inexplicably, an elusive harmony. During the day, in full sun, the garden has all the gaiety of the flamboyant magentas, pinks, reds, oranges, and purples in the phlox, zinnias, trumpet lilies, rudbeckia, montbretia, and Russian sage. Ordinary summer squash vines, with their large yellow blossoms, are intertwined with vibrant blue morning glories, seemingly in perpetual bloom, or with passionflowers, roses, or purple clematis as they all climb up the archways staggered through the parterres. At twilight, when the mood of the garden is at its most bewitching, 20 theatrical lanterns that Joe knowingly

Left: Summer and winter squash, gourds, and pumpkins are all in the large Cucurbita *family. Shown here are the traditional summer varieties (zucchini, crooknecks, straightnecks, and gold and green scallop) with some less common members of the* Cucurbita *family: a large yellow spaghetti squash in the back of the basket next to the smooth-skinned green 'Chayote' and a long thin-skinned Italian 'Cucuzza', or 'Cocozelle', its diminutive name, that curves over all.*

SUMMER SQUASH

(Cucurbita pepo)

Zucchini, scallop (or pattypan), and crookneck are the main types of quick-growing squash for summer vegetable gardens, and they need at least 80–140 frost-free days to mature. Old-fashioned vine or newer bush varieties are also available.

WHEN
Plant as soon as danger of frost is past, after the soil has been tilled with aged manure and its temperature reaches 70°F.

WHERE
Full sun is recommended, but all types will tolerate some summer shade. Good well-drained soil is mandatory.

HOW
Summer squash is usually grown like cucumbers (page 75) in groups of three in hills, and then thinned to the strongest 1 or 2 plants 4–6 feet apart. Alternately, start 2 to 3 weeks earlier indoors in peat pots (not necessary if growing conditions are right, because squash is fast growing).

CARE
Less watering is necessary than with winter squash (page 146), but the care directions are similar. Fertilize with fish emulsion every 2 weeks until flowers appear.

Preceding pages: *The "picnic house," a wooden gazebo, crowns the uppermost of three levels in Joe and Virginia's city garden, where vines of 'Little Gem' summer squash wrap themselves around the bannister that descends to the second level.* Above: *This garden is mostly in the shade—even in summer—and yet even heat-loving squash grow beautifully because of the skill and gardening tricks of Joe McDonnal, a professional* chef and restaurant proprietor in Seattle. *Twelve arches becoming a covered tunnel of roses (and squash vines) curve through the garden, creating the illusion of a larger garden.* Left: *Japanese silver grass (Miscanthus sinensis 'Cabaret') and the bright orange blossoms of shade-tolerant Crocosmia (C. masoniorum) light up some of the shady corners.*

purchased thanks to his unerring designer's eye (at a Bon Marché department store prop display sale) are turned on all over the garden and add considerably to the ambiance of the garden. In summer, the lanterns are echoed here and there by footlights of bright golds and warm yellows in the heliopsis, coreopsis, marigolds, helianthus, and rudbeckia, and often draw attention to the large clumps of sea holly (*Eryngium maritimum*), with its exotic thistlelike silver-blue flowers, or to the variegated grasses and catttails.

On the eastern side, the blossoms of pear and apple trees, old roses from Joe's mother's garden, and an array of peonies take center stage in spring. A stairway, its bannister covered with the rampant squash 'Little Gem', with its fat, round, yellow, smooth-skinned fruit dangling decoratively from the vine, leads to the lowest level of the garden, past the abundant herb beds and a spectacular collection of pastel irises. Here and there, pots of topiary trellises support different varieties of squash. Joe has found that the pale green pattypan squash, which has smaller, more controllable leaves, is particularly successful when trained as a topiary. The English refer to some *Cucurbita pepo* squash as "vegetable marrow," and indeed there are some delicious English ones in the Wyman-McDonnal squash collection, which altogether includes 22 varieties. All varieties do well even in this somewhat shady garden, as they like the rich, composted soil that has become even richer since "our miniature horse, Viva Yo, has come to live with us."

On the lowest terrace an exotic Japanese fuki (*Petasites japonicus* var. *giganteus*), also called giant sweet coltsfoot, dominates the garden. Its stalks are 6 feet tall, and its 4-foot-wide green leaves are phantasmagoric in the moonlight. This stunning addition to the garden, though fairly rare in the United States, is a larger variety of the highly prized *P. japonicus*, of which the young

flower stems as well as the stalks and flower buds can be eaten. This plant above all others in the garden captures the spirit of the exotic, the unique, and a graceful elegance so characteristic of this garden.

The soft romantic whites, pinks, and blues of spring give way later in the season to a new spectacular theater of summer color where yellow, gold, and brilliant orange hues share the scene with flamboyant pinks, purples, reds, and magentas, all clashing together in noisy enthusiasm and rowdy good cheer. The climbing roses make room for the squash vines encumbered by slim, striped Lebanese zucchinis that have suddenly appeared quite mysteriously, as zucchini is wont to do, overnight and out of nowhere. Yellow, red, and shiny green peppers as pretty as any of the neighboring flowers are suddenly in the limelight.

There is a certain worldly, casual abandon in a garden where fat red 'Celebrity' and 'Early Girl' tomatoes grow unostentatiously as part of a dramatic display of kaleidoscopic color. Although Joe says the look of their garden is that of "a garden that was well kempt and maintained and then suddenly the gardener died," much work goes into creating a garden that is so successfully relaxed.

Eight dark green ceramic pots on top of the ivy-covered retaining wall that serves as one side of the lap pool create one of the most decorative motifs in the garden. Here are numerous varieties of squash chosen for their rampant vines and for the different colors of the vegetables themselves. Some are long and curving, like the cucuzza; others are fat and round or scalloped and light green. There are thin gold straightnecks and pale yellow crooknecks. All hang from the squash vines that intertwine with the ivy swags that have been decoratively trained on garlands of chain. As they swing gently between the pots at 12-foot intervals, their reflections are caught in the dark blue water of the 60-foot-long pool, adding another fanciful note to this creative garden. ◥

The Quintessence
of California

NO PLACE COULD BE MORE QUINTESSENTIALLY Californian than Maggie and Harry Wetzel's lovingly restored Victorian house and its garden high on their hillside overlooking their Alexander Valley Vineyards. The main house is one of three buildings within sight of one another on the hill, a white gingerbread building with wraparound porches that Maggie has appropriately and sparingly bedecked with softly scented old garden roses and the yellow Banksia rose. It was originally built in 1864 by Cyrus Alexander, the first homesteader in the Alexander Valley. The second is a nearby schoolhouse of the same vintage, built in 1869 for the local Alexander Valley children and in the same style as the main house, which the Wetzels bought and had moved to a high point on their property and turned into a comfortable guest house. The oldest house on the property was built by Alexander of adobe bricks in 1849 for his Mexican bride. It too was completely restored as a guest house.

It was the modest adobe structure adjoining the garden that gave the late landscape architect Leland Noel of Santa Rosa his decorative cue for the adobe brick wall of the vegetable garden when he drew up the plans for the Wetzels in 1967. All three buildings provide an authentic connection to California's rich and not-too-distant past. The redwoods, an Astrakhan apple tree, and three fig trees also date back to the time of Cyrus Alexander.

The artichoke, the California vegetable par excellence, nestles along part of the 215-foot-long adobe wall that curves around the vegetable garden. Few plants can issue a warmer invitation to be examined closely than the exquisite Mediterranean vegetable, the globe artichoke (*Cynara scolymus*). Here, its outstretched gray-green fronds reach gracefully over the adobe brick wall and offer a strong visual contrast to the decorative Italianate terra-cotta sculptures that flank the entrances to the garden. Admiring the beauty of the shape of the artichoke, Maggie had it copied in two large sculptures that add a delightfully formal note to the garden.

The 50 or so artichoke plants in the Wetzel garden have found their ideal climate and culture: cool summer

Above: 'Ruby Red' Swiss Chard glistens in the California sun before it is harvested for the basis of Maggie Wetzel's delicious vegetarian lasagna or combined with rice, onions, sorrel, cheese, and bread crumbs for a traditional Provençal main dish. Right. Maggie Wetzel picks from the entrance of one of her 24-foot-long bean tunnels (both 'Blue Lake' string beans and 'Dr. Martin' limas). Maggie's husband, Harry, engineered the design of the tunnel that is strongly supported by 7-foot lengths of rebar driven a foot into the ground

Above: *Some of Maggie Wetzel's vegetable bounty near an old trunk of one of the many coast Live Oaks bordering the garden on the northern side.* Left: *The entrance to the vegetable garden is marked by a wide curving band of artichokes—the quintessential California vegetable. The adobe wall is patterned after the original 1849 adobe on the property (now a guest house) built by Cyrus Alexander, the first Euro-American settler in the Alexander Valley.*

nights, frequent sunny days, and the morning fog that rolls in from the Pacific Ocean. In addition, they are pampered with a heavy annual mulch of compost at the end of their season to ensure that the next year's crop will be as good as the last. The leaves are left on the plants for frost protection until the end of February, when they are cut back to encourage new perennial growth. (For those not living in zone 9, artichoke plants can be covered with burlap much as roses are protected or, where winters are extremely severe, simply grown as annuals.)

Maggie is justly proud of the two recently installed 24-foot-long bean tunnels that span two of the paths. They are supported by semicircular PVC arches reinforced by 7-foot lengths of rebar driven 2 feet into the ground. Most important, coarse string stretched along the arches supports the bean vines. The seeds of 'Dr. Martin' lima beans and 'Blue Lake' string beans are planted at 1-foot intervals, one arch for each variety.

In early spring, at the time when the pattern of the well-mulched beds stands out, the garden is just as beautiful as it is at the height of summer abundance. The winding wall bordered by artichokes on the west curves gracefully into an espaliered pear hedge that delineates the garden on the southern side; a 4-foot-wide path, the other sides. Eight beds with simple geometric shapes fit within the grid of the redwood-bordered paths that are covered with compacted redwood chips. While one of these beds is devoted to a cutting garden and another to peonies, six are devoted to annually rotated vegetables.

In addition to the beans and the artichokes, Maggie grows most of the common vegetables—including tomatoes, cucumbers, squash, spinach, beets, carrots, Swiss chard, melons, lettuce, peas, eggplant, peppers, and asparagus. Brightly colored ceramic markers here and there identify the vegetables in their seedling stages before the beds fill up with the vines and bushes of the produce to come.

Different varieties of lettuce are grown in 11 movable boxes (each 3 feet by 7 feet and 1 foot deep), which allow frequent enriching of the soil between plantings. Instead of planting the lettuce seeds directly in the ground as most California gardeners do, Maggie starts them in the adjacent greenhouse and moves the plants out as soon as the weather is warm enough.

And, finally, the three impressive 45-foot-long rows of raspberry bushes are a source of great enjoyment for family and friends. The dead canes are cut back each year to make room for strong new ones, which emerge in early spring. Maggie's secret for growing her luscious berries is to spread lots of compost and wood ashes in the fall and have this remain during the rainy winter.

Not only the historic trees and buildings but also the Mediterranean plants—especially the prickly pears—give the garden deep ties with California's Latin roots.

ARTICHOKES

(Cynara scolymus)

Artichokes are grown on the West Coast almost exclusively as perennials, but certain varieties such as 'Imperial Star' from Shepherd's grow as true annuals (90–100 days from transplants) and will produce in just one growing season.

WHEN
Start seeds in flats indoors 6 weeks before the last frost date.

WHERE
Always grow in full sun, leaving room for a 3-foot spread. Artichokes need long summers and cool night temperatures. They will grow as perennials where the ground does not freeze hard.

HOW
Sow seeds indoors in a flat of starting mix, ½ inch deep and 2 inches apart. Germination takes 10–14 days in an ideally cool location (60–70°F). When seeds sprout move to a cold frame, a greenhouse, or an area with a strong source of light. Begin hardening off outdoors when seedlings have 2–3 sets of leaves. Transplant into well-mulched, fertile soil 2 feet apart.

CARE
Mulch as protection during very hot weather for moisture retention, and also in late fall when hard frost threatens. Fertilize well in March with 15-15-15 (as Maggie Wetzel does). After harvesting, keep leaves on the plant for protection against cold weather. In January, after all danger of frost is past, cut back to encourage new perennial growth.

The Garden
Melting Pot

RAY AND CYNTHIA LUTE'S GARDEN ON PUGET Sound in Des Moines, Washington, is a fascinating testimony to America's multicultural roots. Cynthia's garden design is above all French inspired and is planted predominantly with her favorite European vegetables, but the situation of the garden is uniquely American. It faces out onto the generous natural beauty of Puget Sound, the northernmost U.S. gateway to the Pacific Ocean.

Cynthia and Ray Lute were attracted initially by the magnificent site. On the western side the shores of their property are washed by the gentle waters of Puget Sound. The view from the second-story windows takes in the entire southwestern-facing vegetable garden, a backdrop of Maury and Vashon Islands in the distance, and a view of the small harbor at Des Moines off to the northwestern side. The garden has the benefit of full sun and is laid out to face south.

Cynthia Lute, an industrial designer for 25 years whose talents in recent years have turned to interior and landscape design, became passionately interested in gardening and cooking when she lived in Switzerland a few years ago. She credits Swiss-Italian friends Urs and

Renata Baumann, whose knowledge and enthusiasm gave her a love of both these domestic arts. It was while cooking and gardening with Renata that she developed both her Italian-French culinary repertoire and her gardening skills. When she returned to this country, she continued to learn by studying and reading.

When the Lutes bought their 1937 house in 1991, there was no garden—only the steps that lead down to a second level, which Cynthia incorporated into her design. "It seemed fitting to design a garden in keeping with the style of the house, that is, a French country farmhouse. A version of a French *potager* [kitchen garden] with gravel paths, boxwood enclosures, and espaliered fruit trees seemed appropriate." She chose to accent the centers of the two outside parterres with cordons of Asian pears, lending a particularly formal, elegant look, while an elephant topiary—for a touch of whimsy—surrounded by concave beds of Russian sage (*Perovskia atriplicifolia*) and catnip (*Nepeta cataria*) crowns the middle parterre. "A permanent structure with definite shapes is very important in this garden, particularly since the winters are so long." The yews, hornbeam, and other evergreens

Above: *On the lowest terrace at the bottom of the garden, 'Red Knight' scarlet runner beans and purple climbing hyacinth beans (Dolichos lablab) share one of the antique wrought-iron pillars of an uncovered gazebo.* Right: *Standard 'Iceberg' roses punctuate the centers of the parterres where Russian sage (Perovskia atriplicifolia) fills in among the 'Royal Burgundy' bush beans. A blue atlas cedar (Cedrus atlantica 'Glauca') towers in the background.*

Left: *Asian pears* (Pyrus pyrifolia *and* P. ussuriensis), *a sweet juicy cross between apples and pears, are grown in the Lute garden as espaliered cordons and as standards. Shown here is 'Nijisseiki', one of the most popular varieties grown in the Pacific Northwest.*

Right: *Cynthia Lute uses apple trees including 'Winesap' and 'Gravenstein', which when trained along horizontal supports called "cordons" help emphasize the geometric order of the garden.*

help define the parameters of the garden, and the box-wood and other subshrubs such as lavender and san-tolina, which remain green in winter, provide the interest when the vegetables and flowers are gone. "You need structure to back up the perennials, and the vegetables are very much enhanced by the framing of boxwood around them."

In the Lute garden the symmetry is deliberately con-tradicted by the imbalance of three parterres instead of two, all of equal size, and through the irregular place-ment of the odd-numbered towers and trellises. Strong verticals of 'Delicious' and 'Gravenstein' cordoned apple trees and rectilinear beds running east-west further emphasize the geometry of the garden and are under-planted with nasturtiums and successive plantings of let-tuce, carrots, and radishes. Nevertheless, the beautifully grown vegetables all crowded together and spilling out of their boxwood confinement onto the gravel paths pro-vide the informality that keeps the garden from being strictly in the grand French classical tradition. Finally, the large blue atlas cedar (*Cedrus atlantica* 'Glauca'), used in formal French gardens frequently at the end of a long vista, is another reminder of European gardens. Yet here it stands dramatically off to the side, allowing the expansive view of Puget Sound and the islands beyond to arrest the eye as the main focal point.

Sharing the limited space in each of the parterres are some of Cynthia's beans-for-drying collection from Shepherd's Garden Seeds: 'Midnight Black Turtle', the Italian 'Borlotto', flageolet 'Chevrier Vert', and the tiny 'Astrelle' mini French string bean, which Cynthia also dries for winter use. To all these bush beans she adds from Nichols Garden Nursery their 'Roma' bush beans and the beautiful 'Royal Burgundy Purple' bush bean from Territorial Seed Company (see Source List). Nearby in early spring willow trellises support tiny French *petits*

BEANS

(Phaseolus vulgaris)

Call them string, snap, green, filet, wax, or French beans—*haricots verts*, as the French call them, are the most popular and best-known kind of bean, distinguished from shelling beans in that they are picked when their pods swell and are eaten when young and tender, pod and all.

WHEN
Plant seeds outdoors when the soil temperature is at least 60 degrees and there is no danger of frost.

WHERE
Plots should receive at least half a day of sun.

HOW
Sow bush beans 4 inches apart and 1 inch deep in long or short rows. When seedlings have 2 sets of leaves, thin to 18 inches. Repeat plantings every 2–3 weeks during the summer (provided the weather is not too hot) to increase the crop and to spread the har-vest over a longer period. Plant 5–6 pole beans 1 inch deep and 4–6 inches from each pole. Thin to the strongest 4–6 seedlings.

CARE
Avoid pole-bean root damage by setting trellises up when seedlings are still very young, to provide immediate support. Keep beds well composted, and the soil moist and weed free.

pois (garden peas), and later, when they have gone by, their decorative trellises will be replaced by early and late pickling or 'Kirby' cucumbers, which Cynthia turns into delicious *cornichons* (gherkins). They are harvested daily when they are no more than 2 inches long and stored in the refrigerator with salt until enough have been collected to fill a jar. (Cynthia's pickling ingredients are water, white vinegar, garlic, tarragon, and a little alum, which adds to the crispness of the pickles.)

Four towers for the 'Emerite' *haricots verts* (green beans), Italian 'Romano' pole beans, and the Spanish 'Meralda' pole beans balance the outermost parterres and are underplanted with a variety of lettuces, including green and red 'Oakleaf' and the Italian heirloom 'Red Perella', also from Shepherd's.

In July tomatoes, both 'Early Girl' and 'Oregon Spring', a variety that does particularly well in the Pacific Northwest, are up and fruiting. Their foliage hides the unsightly leaves of the 'Walla Walla' and 'Borettana Italian' heirloom onions when they turn yellow and are dying back underneath.

Luscious basil is underplanted and seeded, as Cynthia learned from an Italian gardener, in trenches over a heavy layer of fertilizer and then thinned out. In nearby parterres, cages of 'Sweet 100' tomatoes diagonally balance a thickly planted bed of fennel, one of the Lutes' favorites, on one side of the path and, on the other,

Left: The view of Puget Sound with Maury and Vashon Islands on the horizon offers a spectacular backdrop for the Lute vegetable garden. Lines created by a softly flowering cosmos hedge and lateral branches of the Atlas cedar repeat the natural horizontals of both the blue sliver of the Sound and the strip of low-slung islands in the distance. Overleaf: Interplanted with tomatoes along the east-west arms of the two Greek cross beds are gherkin cucumbers and a lively climbing summer squash, 'Zucchetta Rampicante', on decorative willow trellises.

symmetrically balanced beds of eggplant and peppers.

The pots of pink and white pelargoniums placed on the uppermost of the three terraces echo the pink and white of the standard roses: 'Dorothy Perkins', 'Iceberg', and 'Seafoam', whose blooms repeat throughout the summer in the centers of the three boxwood parterres on the next level down. These are often highlighted by the different shades of pink in the sky at sunset, purposefully bringing both the sky and its reflections in the water right into the garden scene.

The latitude of this part of Washington is the same as that of Bangor, Maine, and Duluth, Minnesota, yet it is in zone 8 because of the Puget Sound's warming effect exerted by the Pacific's currents and is particularly conducive to growing beautiful vegetables in a long growing season, from mid-March to mid-November. Cynthia says, "Our success is based on an abundance of water and fertilizer [16-16-16 in the spring and a once-a-month application of liquid fertilizer during the growing season]." She believes that the real answer to her successful garden is in the chlorine-free and salt-free processed sewer sludge called "black gold" that she orders and has delivered from the sanitation department for around $15 a cubic yard. In many areas of the country, only a few conservation-minded gardeners have realized the enormous benefits of using processed sewage sludge. It is still possible to obtain this rich organic fertilizer, sometimes even without charge, by inquiring at the local sanitation department.

In conclusion, it is Cynthia's ingeniousness in creating a rich, protective environment for her plants together with her fertile imagination in designing a garden that, though steeped in European tradition, reflects a sense of forward thinking and practical know-how that makes her garden so uniquely American.

A Beautiful
Vegetable
Garden Guide

GROWING TIPS FROM THE GARDENERS

Many gardening handbooks give the basic techniques for making a vegetable garden that produces healthy vegetables, but the needs of a beautiful garden are often specialized. Below are some of the favorite methods and ideas developed by the gardeners in this book especially for ornamental vegetable gardens.

CONTAINER GARDENING

Laurie Eichengreen (pages 60–65)

Twenty years ago, I fell in love with houseplants and realized that almost anything can be grown in a container that can be grown in the ground. Ideally, the shapes and sizes of containers should be selected and customized to fit the specific garden. After many years of working in a small space, though, I have discovered that I have three favorite containers that work for almost everything:

1. The ordinary oak whiskey barrel, 22 inches in diameter by 18 inches high, is perfect for mixing flowers and vegetables in the same container.

2. The large cedar planter, 30 by 30 by 24 inches high, is excellent for terrace trees.

3. The longer planter box, 24 inches by 5 feet by 18 inches high, is the best for a long, narrow space.

Karen Strohbeen (pages 122–127)

One of the best ways to start a vegetable garden is with boxes, because it's like working in a convent or monastery. It's a place for meditation, for focus. You can deal with each box on its own, complete it, and have the satisfaction of having finished something. I got the box idea from an Ortho book called *All About Vegetables*. In the beginning we filled only a few boxes with compost, sand, and soil. The vegetables did well, and we had no trouble controlling the small planting. Also, it's easy to remember where to rotate the vegetables from year to year. Now we work with more than 50 boxes.

Hannah Wister and Teo Gonzales (pages 72–75)

Cucumbers can take over the garden, so we plant ours in 12-by-12-inch pots. Then when the sun gets too hot for them, we can move them to a different location. Each pot takes four vines, which are trained up four stakes tied at the top. For fertilizer, we bury a chunk of aged manure in each pot, but otherwise they don't need anything else all summer. And cutworms never find them.

DESIGNING BY COMPUTER

Jan Moss (pages 22–27)

When I leave my garden in Maine and go back to my apartment in Manhattan, I keep on gardening—on my computer. I already have all the names and addresses for the sources of each plant, subdivided by vegetables, herbs, and flowers. When I travel and when I look at seed catalogs I gather more information, and when I sit down to start my design for next season, I aways start by entering in the past season's successes and failures. I sort the flowers by color so that I know how many yellows and blues I have, and by height—low growing, medium, and tall. With this information I use little pieces of colored papers chosen to match the colors of the flowers and vegetables, and I lay out the garden as a big jigsaw puzzle. I have used the colored papers for years, but it is the computer that has turned out to be the most wonderful help to the garden.

FERTILIZER

Ann and Sigurd Anderson
(pages 128–134)

In addition to processed turkey manure and the organic material we use to enrich the soil when we are preparing the beds, we also add a layer of 8-10-8 fertilizer every time we plant. Then when the vegetables are up, we put against the rows additional fertilizer that is lower in nitrogen, well balanced, and organically based. Because we repeat plantings in the same spot to keep the garden beautiful, because we plant in in-ground containers, and because our growing season is short, we have to keep adding nutrients to the soil to keep production coming. I even add Epsom salts to help keep the plants green. And with so much fertilizer (and our wind conditions), we do need to keep watering.

Marcia Mussman (pages 110–113)

For our asparagus, we use organic compost, pepped up with aged manure from our chickens. Once a year in March, I clean out the previous year's stalks and spread a generous helping of wood ashes and bonemeal. In late spring, the entire bed is covered with a fresh supply of mulch, about 4 to 6 inches deep, usually of grass clippings, but sometimes shredded leaves, depending on what I have the most of.

GARDEN EDGING

Jon Wood and Frank Oatman
(pages 52–57)

Once the site for the garden has been determined and the "frame" is in place, install around the garden wherever weed or grass invasion is a possibility a 1-foot-deep edging of water-resistant boards such as hemlock, buried so that only about 1 to 1½ inches of board shows above the soil. Alternatively, the edging could be of a heavy-duty plastic, or metal. Once all the weeds are eliminated from the actual gardening space, invasion by stolons of such pests as Johnson grass (or witch or crab) is checked, making future maintenance infinitely easier.

PROTECTING YOUNG PLANTS

John Swan (pages 66–71)

Several years ago we discovered that if we took the 6-inch black plastic cans that many nursery owners use for their perennial plants, cut the bottoms out, and sank them into the soil about 2 inches, they protected young transplants not only from wind damage but also from the cutworms that delight in

severing the tender young stems if these are left unprotected. The plastic also acts as a heating element in early spring, when the soil is apt to be on the cold side. Finally, the unobtrusive bottomless containers help direct watering to the plant roots, leaving very little wasteful runoff. Our peppers seem to sit there without growing—just developing their roots for two to three weeks no matter what the weather is like.

SEEDS

Julia Richards (pages 102–109)

Several years ago, we learned the hard way that discount seeds don't pay off. We bought locally at cut-rate prices one year and got only 1 percent germination. Everything had to be replanted. Now we only order from reliable sources.

STARTING PLANTS IN THE GREENHOUSE

Jon Wood and Frank Oatman
(pages 52–57)

In zone 3 every day after Memorial Day is a lost day if your plants are not in the ground, because you only have until

Labor Day for the frost-free season. You have to find the early-growing varieties of every vegetable you plant. We find that broccoli, Brussels sprouts, and usually peas do very well here. We also get enough carrots and cauliflower to freeze for the winter.

Karl Kohring (pages 28–30)

Timing is everything for celery, and my process has four carefully timed steps:

1. I plant celery seeds in early July in the greenhouse in 50-cell plug trays.

2. By August 1, the celery seedlings are transplanted into cement-encased cold frames, where they continue growing uncovered in the fresh air until after the first frost. The transplants are planted equidistantly on 12-inch centers, forming a uniform grid throughout the cold frame.

3. After the first frost, or around October 1, the celery is covered with wooden window sashes, and it remains covered until the first of November.

4. From November 1 until Thanksgiving, I lay plywood over the glass window frames, cutting the stalks off from both sunlight and water. This step blanches the celery, ensuring that it will be crisp and flavorful, and creamy white in color.

Growing celery is really quite simple. It is the delayed planting and manipulations that produce good results.

Hannah Wister and Teo Gonzales (pages 72–75)

Eggplant needs 90 days once the plants have been put into the ground, but they don't like the 90-degree heat waves that hit us in the summer. To make sure that they will be well on their way at transplanting time, and will still be ready to harvest before the frost arrives, we keep them in the greenhouse for an extra 10 to 20 days after the other vegetables have been planted out. Peppers like six hours of sunshine, but eggplants are happy with four, so when we are ready to transplant, we put them among the tomatoes to give them some shade.

VEGETABLE GARDEN BASICS

Juanita Flagg (pages 48–51)

Vegetables are very generous. As long as four basic needs are met, they will give and give:

1. Choose a sunny, open location accessible to water and away from trees, which will rob the soil of moisture and nutrients.

2. If you live in a suburban or rural area, and there is the likelihood of pests such as deer, rabbits, or woodchucks, the garden should be enclosed by either a fence or a wall.

3. Make sure the soil is reasonably fertile, has good drainage, and is at the appropriate pH. Consult your local state farm advisory service and have your soil tested about every two years.

4. Compost—leaves and raw vegetable scraps—is an invaluable resource for healthy soil.

WIND PROTECTION

John Swan (pages 66–71)

Since wind whipped up by thunderstorms is the main foe of our garden, we add protection when the foliage is really well developed. We make our own specially designed cylindrical cages, 18 inches in diameter, of strong concrete with reinforcing wire mesh. We snip off the bottom horizontal wires, leaving the 6-inch vertical prongs to stick into the ground and stabilize the cages. Depending on the height of the plant, the cages can be up to 48 inches in height. Eventually the foliage grows through the mesh and you can't even see the cages.

FAVORITE VEGETABLES OF THE GARDENERS

Choosing the right varietals can sometimes make the difference between an ordinary vegetable garden and a beautiful one. Experiment with these favorites, using the methods that the gardeners in this book rely on to achieve success.

ARTICHOKES
(see page 159)

Tips

If plants look tired, divide and transplant about every third spring. If covered with a mulch after first frost and also with a large basket, artichokes can overwinter in northern zones.

Varietals

Cook's 'Violetto' is hardier than the ordinary 'Green Globe' variety and is also recommended for northern areas above zone 8 if started indoors 8–12 weeks before the last frost.

ASIAN GREENS
(see page 24)

Tips

Enrich the soil before planting with Gardens Alive fertilizer (see Source List).

Varietals

Shepherd's offers 'Tat-soi' as well as 'Mei Qing Choi Pak Choi'. For the flower-bud types, Jan Moss prefers Johnny's 'Hon Tsai Tai' and 'Autumn Poem'. 'Joi Choi', a beautiful cold- and heat-tolerant hybrid variety, and the tender, "baby" Pak Choi 'Mei Qing Choi' are also offered by Johnny's. Mizuna, the mildest of the Oriental greens, can be obtained from Johnny's and Shepherd's.

ASPARAGUS
(see page 113)

Tips

Do not cut spears the first year. Let plants turn to fern, keep them watered well into fall, and let them die back. For white asparagus, continue mounding up soil around the spears to keep them blanched. Cut spears deep under the soil.

Varietals

'Jersey Knight', an all-male strain, and 'Purple Passion' are available through Stark Brothers. Henry Field's and Gurney's offer the classic 'Mary Washington' and 'Hybrid Waltham' as well as 'Hybrid Jersey Giant'.

BEANS
(see page 163)

Tips

In short-summer regions, bush beans usually mature faster than vining types. In hot-summer areas, start beans early in a greenhouse. Daily harvesting will keep vines producing. Pick pods when they are about 3 inches long—think tender and slender. Dust seeds just before planting with a bean/pea inoculant from Cook's to keep beans healthy and disease free.

Varietals

For string bean bush and pole varieties 'Emerite' and 'Trionfo Violetto' from Cook's and 'Kentucky Wonder' and 'Blue Lake' from Harris and Burpee are available.

BROCCOLI
(see page 54)

Tips

At Stones Throw, the garden is enriched annually with a mixture of compost, cow manure, peat moss, green sand, lime, and Pro Gro (an organic fertilizer), which is applied in the fall and turned in the spring before planting.

Varietals

For most zones, including the warm ones, 'Premium Crop' from Harris, Nichols, or Shepherd's is recommended. 'Green Comet' from Harris is early and heat tolerant; Park's 'Early Emerald Hybrid' is described as "the earliest broccoli ever," and Cook's 'Super Dome (Hybrid)' grows well in Vermont. 'Green Lance' Gai Lon and broccoli raab are both available through Shepherd's.

BRUSSELS SPROUTS
(see page 121)

Tips

Harvest from the bottom of the stalk toward the top when sprouts have reached at least the size of a walnut. Pick leaves off below the sprout to encourage continued growth of other sprouts. After picking the lower stem, mound dirt around the base of the plant to prevent toppling over. Use Dipel or nontoxic Bt (*Bacillus thuringiensis*) to control caterpillar pests.

Varietals

'Prince Marvel' from Harris Seeds and Territorial Seed is an early type (76 days). 'Jade Cross' from Pinetree Garden Seeds is Bruce's favorite.

CABBAGES
(see page 130)

Tips

Pests can be controlled with daily inspection and hand collection; a solution of Dipel or Diazinon can help if the problem persists.

Varietals

The Vermont Bean Seed Company offers all types— early middle and late late—including the green and red "ball" varieties, the conical-shaped 'Early Jersey Wakefield', the blue-green 'Grand Slam Hybrid', as well as Savoy and several Chinese varieties.

CARROTS
(see page 139)

Tips

Thin several times during the growing season as soon as seedlings are large enough to be grasped. Thin again when finger size, harvesting the small thinnings for beta carotene nibblings. Plants should stand 2–4 inches apart in the garden. Plant radishes, which will sprout in a few days, next to this slow-germinating vegetable to indicate where the carrots have been seeded. Time carrot plantings in warm-summer zones so they will mature in spring and fall—flavor deteriorates in hot weather.

Varietals

'Imperial Chantenay' from Shepherd's is a stocky variety that grows to about 4–5 inches long and is a favorite in the McDuffie garden. Harris Seeds offers

several popular varieties of pelleted carrot seeds, which are easy to plant and need only minimum thinning. For baby or mini carrots, order 'Planet' and the new French 'Amsdor' from Shepherd's.

CAULIFLOWER
(see page 37)

Tips

If the plants are exposed to too much cold, the cauliflower curds won't develop properly and the heads won't mature. Unseasonable summer rains and too warm nights can cause plants to bolt prematurely. To control cutworms, which are prevalent in early-spring, use biodegradable collars (made from cardboard paper-towel rolls or from newspaper) around each plant, and drench the soil with Diazinon at planting time. Rotate plants to different beds each year to further prevent disease.

Varietals

In addition to white cauliflower, decorative green and purple varieties originally from Italy are commonly available through Johnny's and other seed catalogs.

CELERY
(see page 30)

Tips

Unless a steady temperature of 65–70 degrees is maintained, germination of most varietals may not take place. Blanch non-self-blanching varieties by tying brown paper bags around the stalks or by mounding up the soil around the celery as it grows aboveground. Karl composts his garden with a good application of aged manure in early spring before the celery plants are set out. This enrichment is enough for his successful celery crop. Some gardeners, however, find it helpful to continue a liquid-fertilizer program once a month during the entire growing season.

Varietals

Among celery varieties, 'Golden Self-Blanching' from Nichols, Pinetree Garden Seeds, or Seeds Blum and 'Fordhook Giant' from Seeds Blum (which is shorter and earlier than others) are recommended. Popular varieties of celeraic include 'Prague' from Seeds Blum, 'Large Prague' from Pinetree Garden Seeds, and the Dutch variety 'Mentor' from Shepherd's.

CUCUMBERS
(see page 75)

Tips

A chunk of aged manure in the center of the well-composted soil mixture is all the fertilizer Teo Gonzales's cucumbers need for the entire growing season. Growing cucumbers in containers deters both cutworms and cucumber beetles as well as saves space.

Varietals

'Sweet Success' from Burpee is quite digestible. Shepherd's offers the long Japanese cucumber 'Early Perfection' and the tiny French 'Cornichon' variety (which Cynthia Lute grows so abundantly in Washington's zone 8) as well as the heirloom Armenian variety 'Yard Long Cucumbers'.

KALE & COLLARDS
(see page 105)

Tips

Harvest outer leaves when they reach 2–3 inches long. Continue picking outer leaves through the summer until heat causes bolting. Pull overmature plants when they begin to bolt. A pesto topping for pasta or bruschetta can be made by blanching, chopping, and puréeing kale with garlic and oil.

Varietals

Julia and Ron Richards like 'Champion' collards and 'Southern Giant' mustard seeds from L.L. Olds and

'Vates Dwarf Blue Curled Scotch' from Seeds Blum. Amos Rogers buys local Wyatt-Quarles mustard and collard seeds in North Carolina. Shepherd's offers both the beautiful 'Red Russian', an American heirloom, and the blue-green Dutch variety 'Verdura'.

LETTUCE
(see page 81)

Tips

Where summers are excessively hot, provide covering or additional shade, which can be afforded by companion plants such as pole beans or by planting on the shady side of tomatoes. Manure is the best organic fertilizer to use to supply nitrogen, which is necessary for a steady growth of healthy green leaves.

Varietals

Peggy McDonnell favors 6 varietals from Shepherd's; see page 81 for specific names.

OKRA
(see page 85)

Tips

Soak seeds 8–12 hours to encourage germination.

Varietals

Harris Seeds and Ferry-Morse Seeds are sources for 'Clemson Spineless'. Harris offers the decorative, deep red 'Burgundy' variety. Ferry-Morse carries the dwarf variety 'Emerald', which produces prolific okra pods on short stalks. An early variety that is the most reliable for short-season areas is 'Annie Oakley II' from Johnny's.

ONIONS
(see page 19)

Tips

Match the right variety to the area's or zone's day length. Onions are either short- or long-day cultivars: southern are short-day, such as 'Granax' ('Vidalia'); northern are long-day, such as 'Walla Walla'. Use a well-balanced organic fertilizer or Pro Gro at planting time to get plants off to a good start. Plant young eggplants underneath the foliage of curing onions to take advantage of the shade, as is done in the Wister garden. Green stems mean bulbs are still growing. Don't harvest until the tops are completely brown and the leaves have turned yellow and folded over on the ground. Braid plant leaves for easy hanging in the kitchen and for a decorative touch.

Varietals

Joy Lyons starts the 'Ebenezer' variety from Nichols sets and the large 'Lancastrian' sweet onion from Thompson & Morgan seeds. 'White Lisbon' scallion and 'Golden Gourmet' shallot seeds come from Thompson & Morgan seeds.

PARSNIPS
(see page 45)

Tips

Soak seeds overnight to encourage germinaton. Remember that seeds are short lived, do not keep from year to year, and should be refrigerated until planted. Place a piece of wood or moist burlap on top of the seeds to keep them damp until they begin to sprout. Plant near or under shade-providing companions to ensure continued moisture in the soil.

Varietals

'All American Parsnip' from Nichols and 'Lancer' from Johnny's are recommended.

PEPPERS
(see page 69)

Tips

The Swans apply a rich mushroom compost on their entire garden in the fall and do not need other fertilizer at planting time. Other gardeners spread dehydrated chicken manure at least 12 inches deep before planting and incorporate a handful each of bonemeal and kelp meal into each planting hole. If side-dressing is necessary during the growing season, use a well-balanced fertilizer low in nitrogen.

Varietals

'Cubanelle' and 'Pepperoncini' (the Swans' favorite sweet peppers) are available from Tomato Growers Supply Company, as well as are some of their favorite hot varieties ('Anaheim', 'Ancho', 'Nu Mex Joe E. Parker', 'Jalapeño M', and 'Thai'). 'Cadice' from Shepherd's and 'Golden Bell' from Territorial Seed are also recommended, as well as the large selection from Stokes.

SALSIFY
(see page 99)

Tips

Avoid root splitting by moistening the ground consistently. For easy harvesting, dampen the soil before digging salsify. Frost enhances the flavor. Season lightly, as salsify is the most delicately flavored of all root vegetables.

Varietals

'Sandwich Island Mammoth', the heirloom salsify that Darrell Spencer grows at Old Salem, is offered by Landreth Seed Company, the oldest seed company in the country, as well as by Pinetree Garden Seeds, Seeds Blum, and Johnny's. 'Lange Jan' is a new Belgian variety of scorzonera from Johnny's.

SNOW PEAS
(see page 95)

Tips

Start checking for ripe snow and snap peas 3–4 weeks after flowers appear. Harvest snow peas anytime pods appear; plants will continue to produce as long as harvesting continues, but if seeds form, production will stop.

Varietals

Shepherd's 'Super Sugar Mel' and 'Short 'n' Sweet' from Park Seed.

SPINACH
(see page 51)

Tips

New Zealand, Malabar (Indian), or summer spinach is a good summer substitute for those who want spinach year-round; it is best when cooked because the raw leaves are not very tender.

Varietals

'Melody' from Park Seeds, Nichols, or Harris and the smooth-leaved 'Wolter' and heat-tolerant 'Nordic IV' from Shepherd's also extend the season further into warmer weather.

SUMMER SQUASH
(see page 151)

Tips

Give bushes enough space for air to circulate to decrease the chance of disease. When harvesting, pick yellow crooknecks and straightnecks when no more than 5 inches long; pick zucchini squash anytime and pick scalloped varieties when 2 to 3 inches in diameter.

Varietals

Pinetree Garden Seed Company carries bush varieties; Cook's has yellow and green varieties of all types, including the exotic vining 'Tromboncino'. 'Black Beauty Zucchini' and 'Yellow Crookneck' from Park's Seeds can be trained as modified topiaries in pots.

SWISS CHARD
(see page 126)

Tips

Plant red chard among flowers for a striking accent (as Karen Strohbeen and Bill Luchsinger do) rather than in conventional rows 12 inches apart. Separate leaves from stems for two different cooking trimings and different tastes. Chard gratinéed with Swiss cheese is a favorite.

Varietals

'Fordhook Giant', 'White King', and 'Burpee's Rhubarb Chard' are available through Stokes. Thompson & Morgan offers 'Rhubarb' and 'Lucullus', another good wide-leafed green variety.

TOMATOES
(see page 65)

Tips

Put compost and aged manure in the bottom of the planting hole, mix it well with a handful of bonemeal to encourage fruit set, and cover with soil before setting plants in. Before setting out indeterminate varieties, install cages or supports to avoid root disturbance later. Two advantages to growing tomatoes in containers (as Laurie Eichengreen does) are that soil-borne diseases are eliminated if sterilized potting soil is used, and that heat builds up in the containers, which the tomato as a warm-season vegetable loves. During the growing season, keep plants from drying out and prevent fruit cracking or blossom rot with an even watering on the ground—not on the foliage. Remove sucker foliage to keep energy directed into 2–3 main stems and to encourage fruit development by providing good ventilation and light at the center of the bush.

Varietals

Tomato Growers Supply Company offers 'Dona' and 'Supersonic', both popular in the northeast. The same firm also carries 'Early Girl' and 'Early Cascade', as well as 'Celebrity', which is popular nationwide because of its adaptability.

WINTER SQUASH AND PUMPKINS
(see page 146)

Tips

Pumpkins do cross-fertilize! If you are using hybrid seeds, there is no guarantee—even if isolated from other varieties—that your seeds from last year's crop will produce the same variety.

Varietals

Molly gets her seeds for white pumpkins such as 'Lumina' and the mini 'Baby Boo' from Shepherd's. Stokes also offers a large collection of pumpkin varieties. For winter squash, Seeds Blum has one of the best selections, including the beautiful 'Queensland Blue', 'Flat White Boer', and 'Silver Bell'.

GARDEN PLANS FOR INSPIRATION

When you evaluate your own landscape to plan a garden, consider color, climate, access to water, the existing natural elements, and the entire view of the vegetable garden—and then create your unique design. Following, six plans for inspiration.

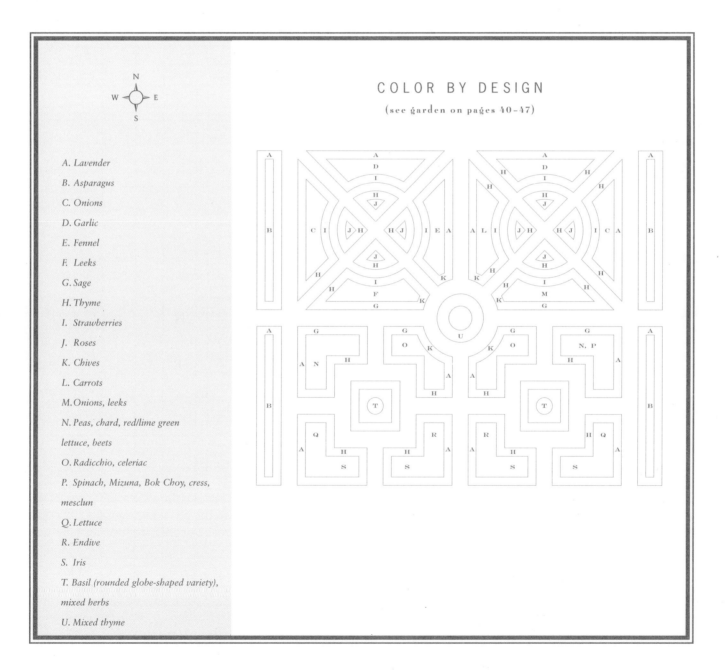

COLOR BY DESIGN
(see garden on pages 40–47)

A. Lavender

B. Asparagus

C. Onions

D. Garlic

E. Fennel

F. Leeks

G. Sage

H. Thyme

I. Strawberries

J. Roses

K. Chives

L. Carrots

M. Onions, leeks

N. Peas, chard, red/lime green lettuce, beets

O. Radicchio, celeriac

P. Spinach, Mizuna, Bok Choy, cress, mesclun

Q. Lettuce

R. Endive

S. Iris

T. Basil (rounded globe-shaped variety), mixed herbs

U. Mixed thyme

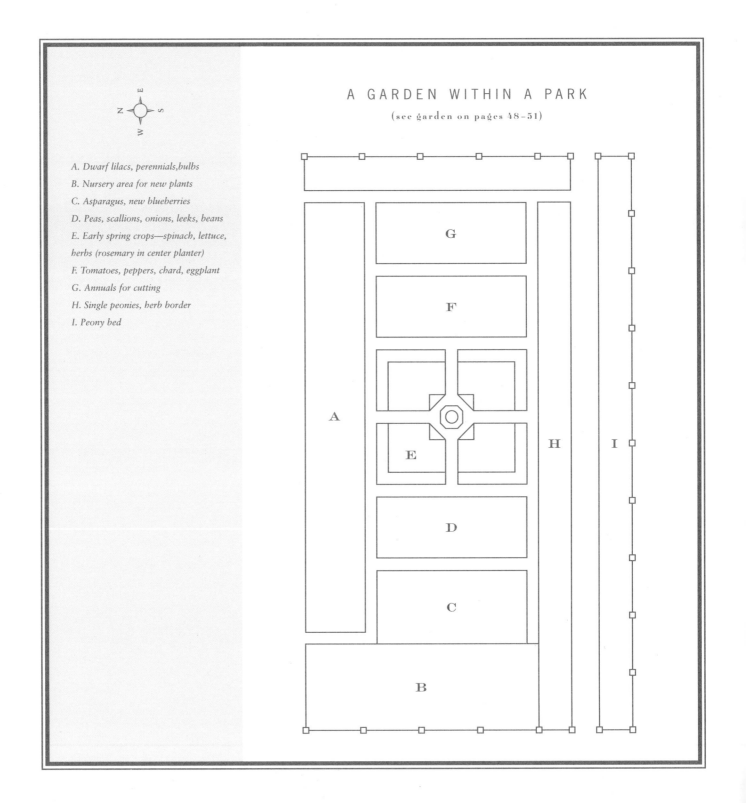

A. Dwarf lilacs, perennials, bulbs

B. Nursery area for new plants

C. Asparagus, new blueberries

D. Peas, scallions, onions, leeks, beans

E. Early spring crops—spinach, lettuce, herbs (rosemary in center planter)

F. Tomatoes, peppers, chard, eggplant

G. Annuals for cutting

H. Single peonies, herb border

I. Peony bed

A GARDEN WITHIN A PARK

(see garden on pages 48–51)

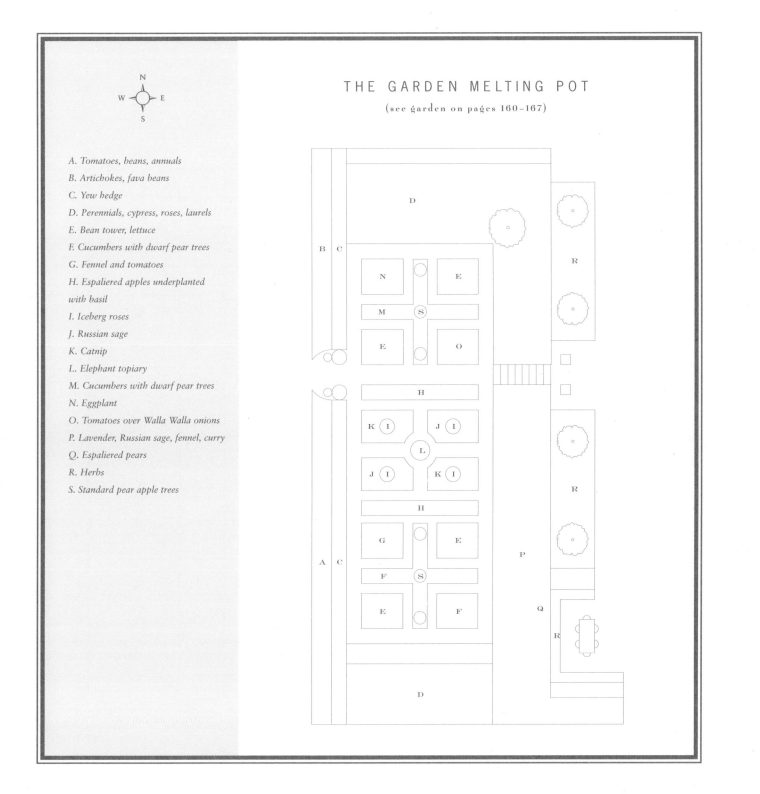

THE GARDEN MELTING POT

(see garden on pages 160–167)

A. Tomatoes, beans, annuals

B. Artichokes, fava beans

C. Yew hedge

D. Perennials, cypress, roses, laurels

E. Bean tower, lettuce

F. Cucumbers with dwarf pear trees

G. Fennel and tomatoes

H. Espaliered apples underplanted
with basil

I. Iceberg roses

J. Russian sage

K. Catnip

L. Elephant topiary

M. Cucumbers with dwarf pear trees

N. Eggplant

O. Tomatoes over Walla Walla onions

P. Lavender, Russian sage, fennel, curry

Q. Espaliered pears

R. Herbs

S. Standard pear apple trees

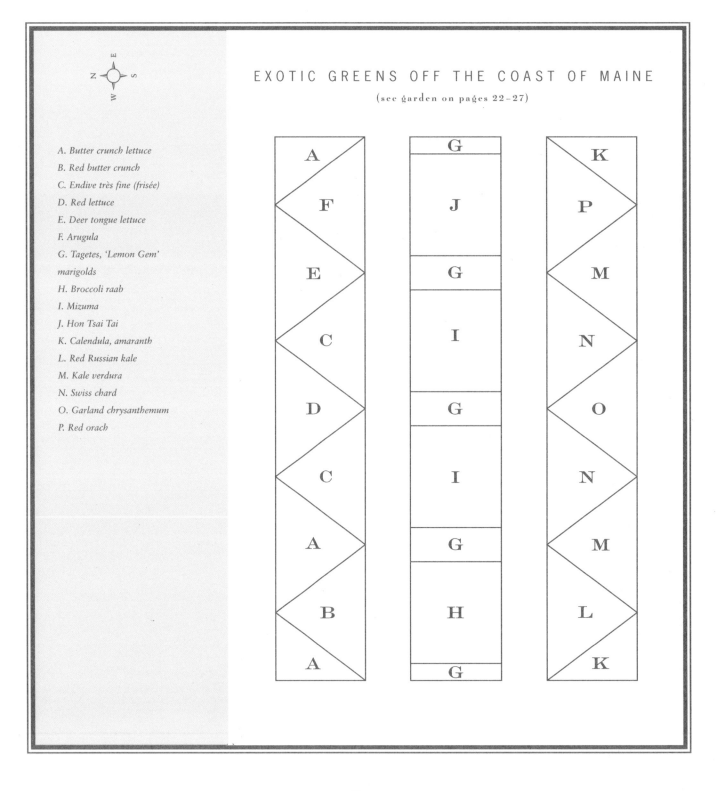

EXOTIC GREENS OFF THE COAST OF MAINE

(see garden on pages 22–27)

A. Butter crunch lettuce

B. Red butter crunch

C. Endive très fine (frisée)

D. Red lettuce

E. Deer tongue lettuce

F. Arugula

G. Tagetes, 'Lemon Gem' marigolds

H. Broccoli raab

I. Mizuma

J. Hon Tsai Tai

K. Calendula, amaranth

L. Red Russian kale

M. Kale verdura

N. Swiss chard

O. Garland chrysanthemum

P. Red orach

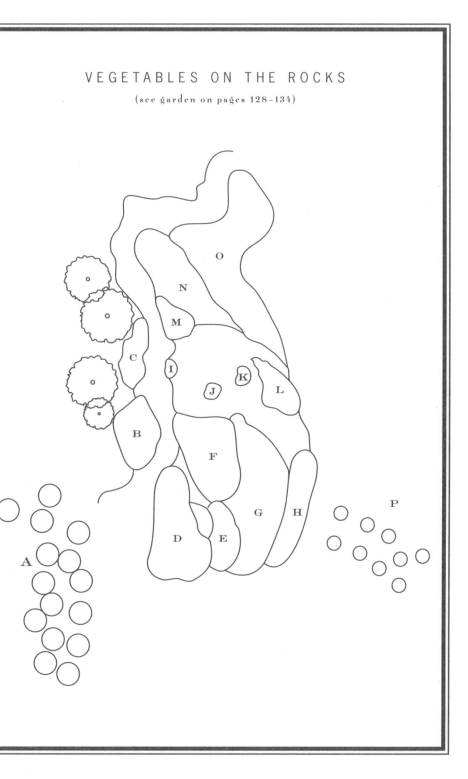

VEGETABLES ON THE ROCKS

(see garden on pages 128–134)

A. Herb garden—basil, Chinese chives, chives, chocolate mint, Italian parsley, lemon thyme, lime mint, old spice mint, orange mint, oregano, rosemary, sage, tarragon, thyme

B. Tomatoes

C. Sharing garden (native tree seedlings in pots)

D. Lettuces: Arugula, cress, endive, 'French Mantilla', 'Green Ice', mâche, radicchio, rhubarb, royal oakleaf, 'Tom Thumb', wild strawberries

E. Red cabbage, 'Ronde de Nice', yellow potatoes

F. Blue, red, and yellow potatoes; Danish cabbage, garlic, scallions, spring raab

G. Basil, golden scallop and butter stick squash, savoy cabbage, broccoli, Italian parsley

H. Italian parsley, basil, cabbage, spinach, beets, broccoli, mounding nasturtium

I. Cucumber

J. Acorn squash

K. Butternut squash

L. Basil, broccoli, red cabbage

M. Kale, leeks, parsley

N. Broccoli, cabbage, red cabbage, pumpkins, cucumber, snow peas, sugar snap peas

O. Eggplant, peppers, ruby and green chard, broccoli, carrots, celery, haricots verts, wax beans, scarlet runner

P. Raspberries

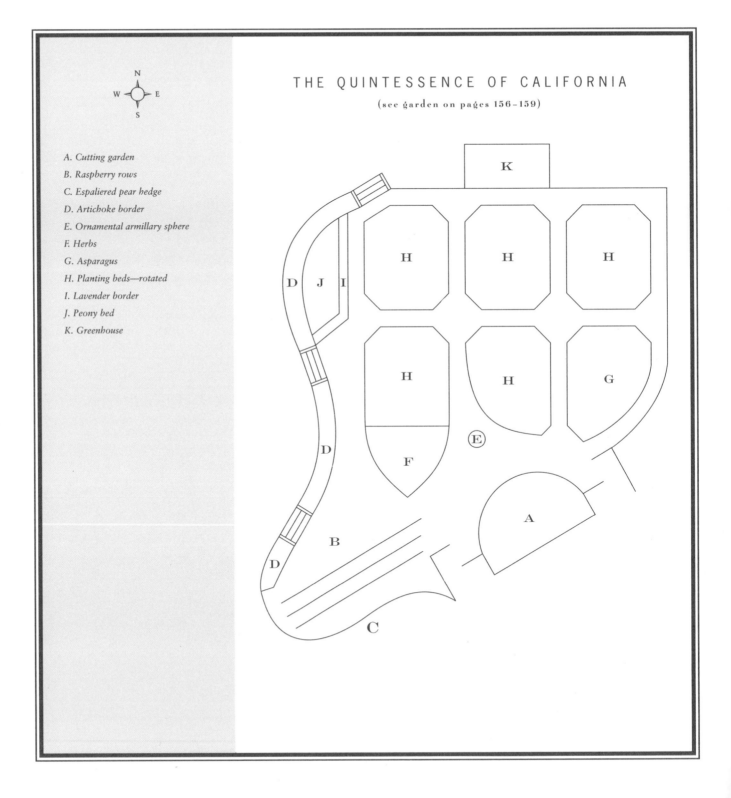

THE QUINTESSENCE OF CALIFORNIA

(see garden on pages 156–159)

A. Cutting garden

B. Raspberry rows

C. Espaliered pear hedge

D. Artichoke border

E. Ornamental armillary sphere

F. Herbs

G. Asparagus

H. Planting beds—rotated

I. Lavender border

J. Peony bed

K. Greenhouse

SOURCE LIST

VEGETABLE SEEDS

Bluebird Nursery, Inc.
519 Bryan
Clarkson, NB 68629
(800) 356-9164
(402) 892-3738 fax
(wholesale only)

W. Atlee Burpee & Co.
Warminster, PA 18974
(800) 888-1447
(800) 487-5530 fax

The Cook's Garden
P.O. Box 535
Londonderry, VT 05148
(802) 824-3400
(802) 824-3027 fax

Earl May Garden Center
208 North Elm Street
Shenandoah, IA 51603
(712) 246-1020
(712) 246-2210 fax
(no mail order)

Fern Hill Farm
P.O. Box 185
Clarksboro, NJ 08020
(609) 423-3889
(for 'Dr. Martin' lima beans)

Ferry-Morse Seed Co.
P.O. Box 488
Fulton, KY 42041
(800) 283-3400
(800) 283-2700 fax

Gurney's Seed and Nursery Co.
110 Capital Street
Yankton, SD 57079
(605) 665-1671
(605) 665-9718 fax

Harris Seeds
60 Saginaw Drive
P.O. Box 22960
Rochester, NY 14692-2960
(716) 442-0100
(716) 442-9386 fax

Henry Field's Seed & Nursery Co.
415 North Burnett
Shenandoah, IA 51602
(712) 665-9391
(712) 665-2601 fax

Johnny's Selected Seeds
Foss Hill Road
Albion, ME 04910

Mellinger's
2310 W. South Range Rd.
North Lima, OH 44452-9731
(216) 549-9861
(216) 549-3716

Nichols Garden Nursery
1190 North Pacific Highway
Albany, OR 97321-4580
(503) 928-9280
(503) 967-8406 fax

NK Lawn & Garden Co.
P.O. Box 24028
Chattanooga, TN 37422-4028
(wholesale only)

L.L. Olds Seed Co.
P.O. Box 7790
Madison, WI 53707-7790
(wholesale only)

Park Seed Co.
Cokesbury Road
Greenwood, SC 29647-0001
(803) 223-7333

Piedmont Plant Co.
P.O. Box 424
Albany, GA 31703
(912) 435-0766

Pinetree Garden Seeds
P.O. Box 300
New Gloucester, ME 04260
(207) 926-3400

Seeds Blum
HC 33 Idaho City Stage
Boise, ID 83706
(208) 338-5658 fax

Shepherd's Garden Seeds
30 Irene Street
Torrington, CT 06790
(203) 482-3638

Stokes
P.O. Box 548
Buffalo, NY 14240-0548
(716) 695-6980
(716) 695-9649 fax

Territorial Seed Co.
P.O. Box 157
Cottage Grove, OR 97424
(800) 626-0866
(503) 942-9881 fax

Thompson & Morgan, Inc.
P.O. Box 1308
Jackson, NJ 08527-0308
(908) 363-2225
(908) 363-9356 fax

Tomato Growers Supply Co.
P.O. Box 2237
Fort Myers, FL 33902

The Vermont Bean Seed Co.
Garden Lane
Fair Haven, VT 05732
(802) 273-3400
(802) 663-9772 fax

Wayside Gardens
1 Garden Lane
Hodges, SC 29695-0001
(800) 845-1124
(803) 941-4206 fax

HEIRLOOM AND HARD-TO-FIND VEGETABLE SEEDS

Abundant Life Seed Foundation
P.O. Box 772
Port Townsend, WA 98368

Bountiful Gardens
5798 Ridgewood Road
Willits, CA 95490

D. Landreth Seed Co.
P.O. Box 6426
Baltimore, MD 21230

Heirloom Seeds
P.O. Box 245
West Elizabeth, PA 15088
Seeds of Change
P.O. Box 15700

Santa Fe, NM 87506-5700
(505) 438-8080
(505) 438-7052 fax

Seed Savers Exchange
3076 North Winn Road
Decorah, IA 52101

Southern Exposure Seed Exchange
P.O. Box 170
Earlysville, VA 22936

Walker Farm
R.D. Box 556
Putney, VT 05346
(802) 254-2476
(802) 254-2051 fax

CURRANTS AND OTHER BERRIES, FRUIT TREES, NUTS

Raintree Nursery
391 Butts Road
Morton, WA 98356
(360) 496-6400

Stark Brothers Nurseries & Orchards
Louisiana, MO 63353-0010
(800) 325-4180
(573) 574-5290 fax

GARDENING EQUIPMENT AND FERTILIZERS

Bosmere, Inc.
P.O. Box 363
323 Corban Avenue S.W.
Concord, NC 28026
(704) 784-1606
(spiral tomato plant supports)

Gardener's Supply Co.
128 Intervale Road
Burlington, VT 05401-2850
(802) 863-1700
(seed starter kits, organic fertilizers, insect repellents, and other supplies)

Gardens Alive
5100 Schenley Place
Lawrenceburg, IN 47025
(812) 537-8650
(812) 537-5108 fax
(for 'Vegetable Alive' fertilizer and other organic gardening products)

Harris Seeds
60 Saginaw Drive
P.O. Box 22960
Rochester, NY 14692-2960
(Jiffy pots, seed starter kits, Wall o' Water plant protectors)

Kinsman Company, Inc.
River Road
Point Pleasant, PA 18950
(800) 733-4146
(excellent tools, cold frames)

Smith & Hawken Ltd.
117 E. Strawberry Drive
Mill Valley, CA 94941
(800) 776-3336
(tools, glass cloches, Wall o' Water plant protectors, and other supplies)

BIBLIOGRAPHY

American Society of Landscape Architects. *Colonial Gardens: The Landscape Architecture of George Washington's Time*. Washington, D.C.: United States George Washington Bicentennial Commission, 1932.

Balmori, Diana, Diane Kostial McGuire, and Eleanor M. McPeck. *Beatrix Farrand's American Landscapes: Her Gardens and Campuses*. Sagaponack, N.Y.: Sagapress, 1985.

Bisgrove, Richard. *The Gardens of Gertrude Jekyll*. Boston: Little, Brown and Company, 1992.

Brown, Jane. *Beatrix: The Gardening Life of Beatrix Jones Farrand, 1872–1959*. New York: Viking, 1995.

Bush-Brown, James and Louise. *America's Garden Book*, rev. ed. by the New York Botanical Garden. New York: Scribners, 1980.

Chappellet, Molly. *A Vineyard Garden: Ideas from the Earth for Growing, Cooking, and Entertaining*. New York: Viking Studio Books, 1991.

Clarkson, Rosetta E. *Magic Gardens: A Modern Chronicle of Herbs and Savory Seeds*. New York: Macmillan, 1942.

Cobbett, William A. *The American Gardener*. London: Clement, 1821.

Crowe, Sylvia. *Garden Design*. Woodbridge, Suffolk, U.K.: Garden Art Press, 1994.

Downing, A. J., III, ed. *Cottage Residences*. New York: Wiley and Putnam, 1847.

———. *Treatise on the Theory and Practice of Landscape Gardening Adapted to North America; with a View to the Improvement of Country Residences*, 6th ed. New York: A. O. Moore, 1859.

Eaton, Leonard K. *Landscape Artist in America: The Life and Works of Jens Jensen*. Chicago: University of Chicago Press, 1964.

Elder, Walter. *The Cottage Garden of America*, 2nd ed., Philadelphia: Moss and Brother, 1850.

Favretti, Rudy and Joy. *For Every House a Garden: A Guide for Reproducing Period Gardens*. Hanover and London: University Press of New England, 1990.

Fitch, James M., and F. F. Rockwell. *Treasury of American Gardens*. New York: Harper and Bros., 1956.

Gainey, Ryan. *The Well-Placed Weed: The Bountiful Garden of Ryan Gainey*. Dallas: Taylor Publishing Company, 1993.

Goldstein, Judith S. *Tragedies and Triumphs: Charles W. Eliot, George B. Dorr, John D. Rockefeller, Jr.: The Founding of Acadia National Park*. Somesville, Maine: Port in a Storm Bookstore.

Griswold, Mac, and Eleanor Weller. *The Golden Age of American Gardens*. New York: Abrams, in association with the Garden Club of America, 1991.

Harper, Pamela, and Frederick McGourty. *Perennials: How to Select, Grow and Enjoy*. Los Angeles: HP Books, a division of Price Stern Sloan, Inc., 1982.

Hedrick, U. P. *A History of Horticulture in America to 1860*. New York: Oxford University Press, 1950.

Hobhouse, Penelope. *Garden Style*. Boston: Little, Brown and Company, 1988.

———. *Gardening through the Ages: An Illustrated History of Plants and Their Influence on Garden Styles—From Ancient Egypt to the Present Day.* New York: Simon and Schuster, 1992.

Jekyll, Gertrude. *A Gardener's Testament.* Woodbridge, Suffolk, U.K.: Antique Collectors Club Ltd., 1982.

———. *Colour Schemes for the Flower Garden.* Woodbridge, Suffolk, U.K.: Antique Collectors Club Ltd., 1990.

———. *Garden Ornament.* Woodbridge, Suffolk, U.K.: Antique Collectors Club Ltd., 1982.

Jellicoe, Geoffrey and Susan, Patrick Goode, and Michael Lancaster. *The Oxford Companion to Gardens.* Oxford: The Oxford University Press, 1986.

Jensen, Jens. *The Clearing: "A Way of Life."* Chicago: R. F. Seymour, 1949.

Lazzaro, Claudia. *The Italian Renaissance Garden.* New Haven: Yale University Press, 1990.

Leighton, Ann. *American Gardens in the Eighteenth Century: "For Use or for Delight."* Amherst: The University of Massachusetts Press, 1976.

———. *American Gardens in the Nineteenth Century: "For Comfort and Afflluence."* Amherst: The University of Massachusetts Press, 1987.

Lockwood, Alice G. B. *Gardens of Colony and State.* New York: Scribners, for the Garden Club of America, 1931–34.

Lounsberry, Alice. *Gardens Near the Sea: The Making and Care of Gardens On or Near the Coast.* New York: Frederick A. Stokes Company, c. 1910.

———. *Gardens by the Sea and Beautiful Homes of Northern N.J.* New York: Scribners, 1910.

Montagné, Prosper. *Larousse Gastronomique: The Encyclopedia of Food, Wine & Cookery.* New York: Crown Publishers, 1961.

Oehme, Wolfgand, and James van Sweden, with Susan Rademacher Frey. *Bold Romantic Gardens: The New World Landscapes of Oehme and van Sweden.* Reston, Va., 1990.

Ottesen, Carole. *The New American Garden.* New York: Macmillan Publishing Company, 1987.

Patterson, Robert W., A.S.L.A. *Beatrix Jones Farrand, 1872–1959: An Appreciation of a Great Landscape Gardener.* Published by Mrs. Robert Woods Bliss Press of Judd and Detweiler, Inc., 1960.

Proctor, Rob. *Annuals: Yearly Classics for the Contemporary Garden.* New York: HarperCollins, 1991.

Rae, John W., and John W. Rae, Jr. *Morristown's Forgotten Past: The Story of a New Jersey Town.* Morristown: privately printed, 1979.

Raphael, Sandra. *An Oak Spring Sylva: A Selection of the Rare Books on Trees in the Oak Spring Garden Library.* Upperville, Va.: Oak Spring Garden Library, 1989.

———. *An Oak Spring Pomona: A Selection of the Rare Books on Fruit in the Oak Spring Garden Library.* Upperville, Va.: Oak Spring Garden Library, 1990.

Roberts, Martha McMillan. *Public Gardens and Arboretums of the United States.* New York: Holt, Rinehart and Winston, 1962.

Rohde, Eleanour Sinclair. *Uncommon Vegetables and Fruits: How to Grow and How to Cook.* London: Country Life Limited, 1951.

Root, Waverly. *Food: An Authoritative and Visual History and Dictionary of the Foods of the World.* New York: Simon and Schuster, 1980.

Rose, Graham. *The Classic Garden.* New York: Summit Books, 1989.

Salon, Marlene. *Beatrix Farrand, Landscape Gardener: Her Life and Her Work.* Thesis, University of California, Berkeley, 1976.

Schneider, Elizabeth. *Uncommon Fruits and Vegetables: A Commonsense Guide.* New York: Harper and Row, 1986.

Schrambling, Regina. *Squash: A Country Garden Cookbook.* San Francisco: Collins Publishers, 1994.

Shelton, Louise. *Beautiful Gardens in America,* rev. ed. New York: Scribners, 1924.

Slade, Daniel Denfson. *The Evolution of Horticulture in New England.* New York and London: Putnam's, 1895.

Slosson, Elvenia. *Pioneer American Gardening.* New York: Coward-McCann, 1951.

Snow, Marc. *Modern American Gardens Designed by James Rose.* New York: Reinhold Publishing Corporation, 1967.

Straw, Jane Anne, and Mary Swander. *Parsnips in the Snow Talks with Midwestern Gardeners.* Iowa City: University of Iowa Press, 1990.

Talbot County Historical Society. *The Art of Gardening: Maryland Landscapes and the American Garden Aesthetic.* Exhibition catalog, Easton, Md.: Historical Society of Talbot County, 1985.

Tice, Patricia M. *Gardening in America, 1830–1910.* Rochester, N.Y.: The Strong Museum, 1984.

Tishler, William, ed. *American Landscape Architecture: Designers and Places.* Washington, D.C.: Preservation Press, 1989.

Trollop, Frances. *Domestic Manners of the Americans* (1832). New York, 1927 (reprint).

Van Renssleleer, Mrs. Schuyler. *Art Out-of-Doors: Hints on Good Taste in Gardening.* New York: Scribners, 1911.

Verey, Rosemary. *Classic Garden Design.* New York: Random House, 1984.

Warner, Anna Bartlett. *Gardening by Myself* (1829). New York: Duffield and Company, 1924.

Washburn and Company *Amateur Cultivator's Guide to the Flower and Kitchen Garden.* Boston: Washburn and Company, Seed Merchants, 1869.

Wilkinson, Elizabeth, and Marjorie Henderson. *Decorating Eden.* San Francisco: Chronicle Books, 1992.

PERIODICALS AND GUIDEBOOKS

Berckman, Julianne. "An 18th-century Kitchen Garden," *Early American Life—Gardens.* Historical Times, Inc., 1988, 30–35.

Brooklyn Botanic Garden Record, Plants and Gardens: American Cottage Gardens. New York, 1990.

Bynum, Flora Ann L., *Old Salem Garden Guide.* Winston-Salem, N.C.: Old Salem, Inc., 1979.

Farrand, Beatrix. "Beatrix Farrand," *Reef Point Gardens Bulletin.* Bar Harbour, Maine: The Max Farrand Memorial Fund, 1946.

Eaton, Leonard K. "Jens Jensen and the Chicago School," *Progressive Architecture,* Dec. 1960, 144–50.

Goldstein, Judith. "Houses, Cottages and Camps: Who Lives in What on Mt. Desert?" Lecture given at Claremont Hotel, Mount Desert Island, Maine, July 13, 1995.

James, Hunter, and Frances Griffin, eds. *Old Salem Official Guidebook*. Winston-Salem, N.C.: Old Salem, Inc., 1993.

Miller, Wilhelm. "The Prairie Spirit in Landscape Gardening: What the People of Illinois Have Done and Can Do Toward Designing and Planting Public and Private Grounds for Efficiency and Beauty." Urbana, Ill.: University of Illinois, Nov. 1915.

Miller, Wilhelm. "Bringing the Country into the City," *Country Life in America*. Sept. 1910, 524–27.

USEFUL REFERENCES

Bradley, Fern Marshall, ed. *Rodale's Garden Answers: Vegetables, Fruits and Herbs*. Emmaus, Pa.: Rodale Press, 1995.

Johns, Glenn F. *The Basic Book of Organic Gardening*. Edited by Robert Rodale. New York: Ballantine Books, 1971.

Ogden, Shepherd, and Ellen Ogden. *The Cook's Garden*. Emmaus, Pa.: Rodale Press, 1989.

Phillips, Roger, and Martyn Rix. *The Random House Book of Vegetables*. New York: Random House, 1993.

Taylor, Norman. *Taylor's Guide to Vegetables and Herbs*. Edited by Gordon P. DeWolf, Jr. New York: Houghton Mifflin, 1987.

The Time-Life Gardener's Guide. *Summer Vegetables*. Alexandria, Va.: Redefinition, Time-Life Books, 1988.

FAVORITE VEGETABLE COOKBOOKS

Allard, Linda. *Absolutely Delicious*. New York: Random House, 1994.

Child, Julia. *The Way to Cook*. New York: Alfred A. Knopf, 1989.

Khalsa, Baba S. *Great Vegetables from the Great Chefs: A Compendium of Recipes and Anecdotes*. San Francisco: Herman and Company, 1990.

LaPlace, Viana. *Verdura Vegetables Italian Style*. New York: William Morrow and Company, 1991.

Larkcom, Joy. *Oriental Vegetables: The Complete Guide for Garden and Kitchen*. London: John Murray, 1991.

Madison, Deborah. *The Greens Cook Book*. Toronto and New York: Bantam Books, 1987.

Morash, Marian. *The Victory Garden Cookbook*. New York: Alfred A. Knopf, 1982.

Scaravelli, Pola, and Jon Cohen. *Cooking from an Italian Garden*. New York: Holt, Rinehart and Winston, 1984.

Waters, Alice. *Chez Panisse Vegetables*. New York: HarperCollins Publishers, 1996.

INDEX

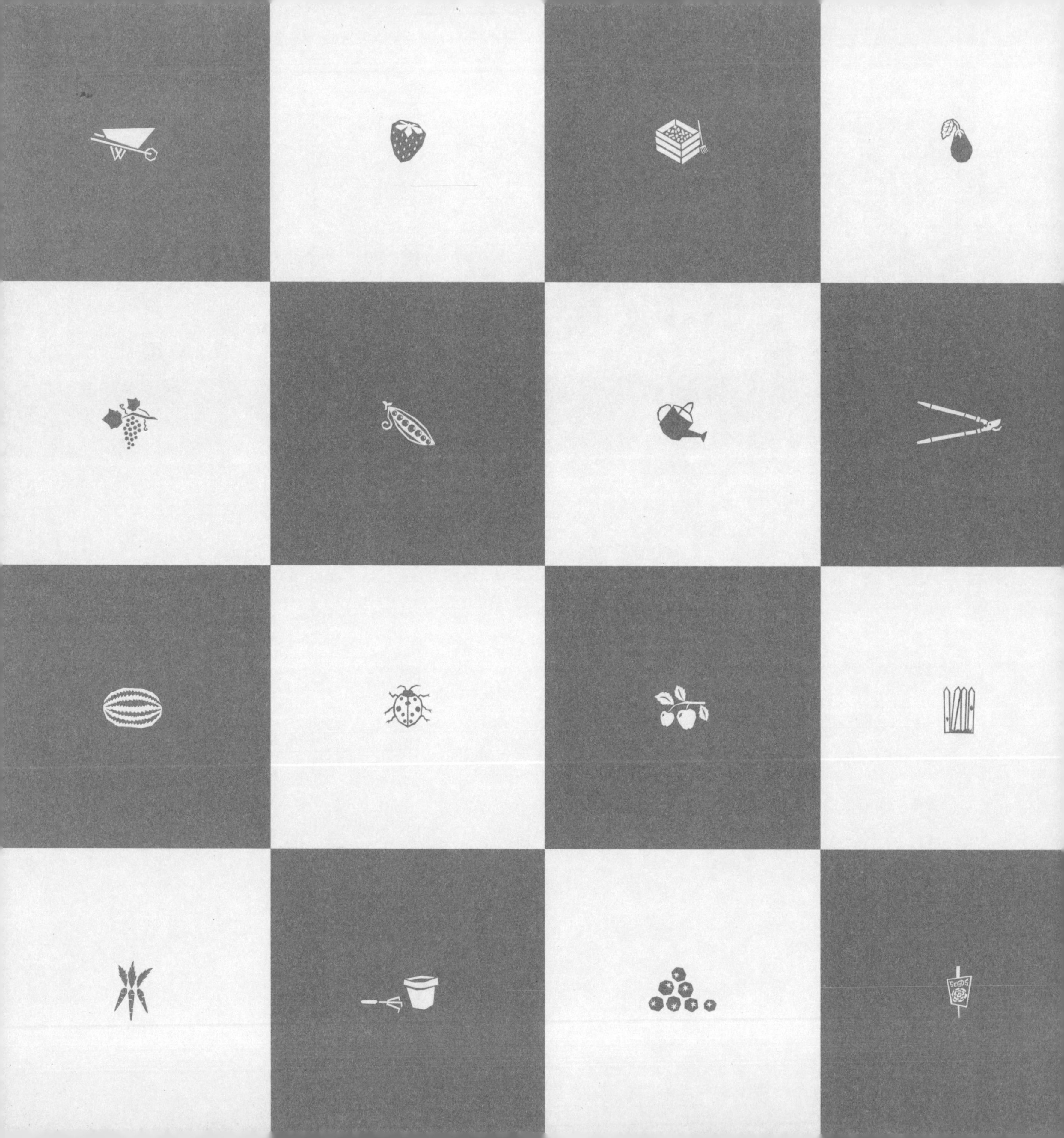
SEEDS